What Dwells Within

A Study of Spirit Attachment

What Dwells Within

A Study of Spirit Attachment

Jayne Harris and D. J. Weatherer

6th BOOKS

Winchester, UK
Washington, USA

First published by Sixth Books, 2015
Sixth Books is an imprint of John Hunt Publishing Ltd., Laurel House, Station Approach,
Alresford, Hants, SO24 9JH, UK
office1@jhpbooks.net
www.johnhuntpublishing.com
www.6th-books.com

For distributor details and how to order please visit the 'Ordering' section on our website.

Text copyright: Jayne Harris and D. J. Weatherer 2014

ISBN: 978 1 78535 032 0
Library of Congress Control Number: 2015930442

A CIP catalogue record for this book is available from the British Library.

Design: Lee Nash

Printed and bound by CPI Group (UK) Ltd, Croydon, CR0 4YY, UK

We operate a distinctive and ethical publishing philosophy in all
areas of our business, from our global network of authors to
production and worldwide distribution.

CONTENTS

For Daisy, Connie, Bethany and Nathan

Introduction

What is spirit attachment if not the very definition of a haunting? It is believed that ghosts haunt areas that the deceased were either fond of or met their demise within, and there are countless volumes dedicated to the documentation of haunted places and the history behind each alleged ghost. Borley Rectory, once dubbed the most haunted house in England allegedly housed numerous spirits before a mysterious fire in 1939 wreaked havoc on the property and rendered it uninhabitable. Glamis Castle is home to a 'grey lady' (so called as her manifestation appears grey to the eye,) whom is often seen kneeling in prayer (Haining, 2008). These are just two of the more famous hauntings in Britain; the list of locations that are reputedly haunted is endless. Indeed there is no culture that does not have its own belief system in place when it comes to explaining the mysteries of life after death. For this reason ghost stories abound the world over.

If a spirit can attach itself to a place that it once shared a connection with, then why not an object? Why not a favoured item of furniture, artwork or a piece of jewellery? If – like many paranormal enthusiasts believe – a building can record the energy or emotions of an individual and replay that incident at a later date (more commonly known as the stone tape theory), why is it improbable that a wedding ring could hold the essence or emotions of the person who once wore it?

Recent box office hits such as *The Conjuring* have thrust the idea of attachment upon an unsuspecting audience with terrifying results. Yet the phenomenon of spirit attachment is not a new concept.

One of the oldest recorded items that allegedly has a spirit attached to it is a statue named 'The Woman from Lemb'. The piece was originally unearthed in the Cypriot town of Lemb in1878. It was carved from pure limestone and was dated at originating from around 3500 BC. It was believed that she symbolised a fertility god popular to the region around that time. The statue came into possession of a man by the name of Lord Elphont, yet within six years of him owning all the statue, all six members of his family had perished in mysterious circumstances.

The idol was then blamed for the deaths of Ivor Manucci and Lord Tompson-Noel along with their entire families, both of whom had owned the statue for a short time.

The piece was eventually donated to the Royal Scottish Museum of Edinburgh by the surviving sons of Sir Alan Riverbrook. It is said that shortly after receiving the statue the curator of the particular section where the statue was displayed, passed away. The statue remains behind thick glass, safely out of reach of human touch. (10 most Haunted Objects of all time, www.oddee.com, 2013.)

Then there is the alleged 'Chair of Death', which formed part of the furniture of a popular Thirsk public house. It is said that in 1702, before his execution, convicted murderer Thomas Busby was granted a last meal at his favourite pub. Upon completing his meal he is said to have uttered the following: *"May sudden death come to anyone who dare sit in my chair."*

The chair remained in the pub for centuries. Careless revellers would often dare each other to take a seat upon the cursed chair and for those that did, death followed quickly.

It was noted that during World War II a lot of the young servicemen who sat in the chair did not return home. Admittedly, this was no great surprise as war tends to claim many of our young. However, in 1967, two Royal Air Force pilots sat in the chair only to crash their truck into a tree on the ride back to base. Both were killed instantly. Then in 1970, a local Mason dared sit in the fabled seat before falling to his death later that day. The cause of death was falling into deep hole on the site where he had been working. A year later, a roofer who had sat on the chair died when the roof he was working on collapsed.

The final straw for the landlord came when his cleaning lady slipped and fell into the chair. She died shortly afterwards, the cause of death this time was a sudden brain tumour.

The chair was moved into the cellar where it was to claim yet another victim when a weary delivery driver took a rest upon it. Later that day he was killed in a car accident.

The chair now resides in a nearby museum, suspended five feet from the ground so that nobody will ever make the fatal mistake of sitting in it again. (10 most Haunted Objects of all time, 2013.)

Chairs feature quite prominently in spiritual attachment. Belfcourt castle, situated in Newport, Rhode Island was built in 1894 for Oliver Belmont and is reputedly home to many lavish antiques. It is said that two chairs in particular have spirits attached to them. Visitors to the castle who have had the unfortunate pleasure of sitting in the chairs have reported feeling uneasy and sick. Others have felt a prickly sensation, as though they have received a form of static shock from them. Less fortunate souls have found themselves ejected forcefully from the chairs by unseen hands. (10 most Haunted Objects of all time, 2013.)

One of the most unnerving aspects of spiritual attachment (at least for some), is when an apparent attachment occurs with a children's doll. In fact the part of the movie *The Conjuring* that discusses the doll Annabelle, is based upon a true story.

A toy that goes by the name of Robert though is arguably the most famous haunted doll of our time. Allegedly given to a young boy named Robert Eugene Otto in Key West, Florida during the summer of 1896 by a Bahamian servant who practiced the dark arts, Robert made an instant impact upon the household. It was said that the young boy would hold conversations with the doll that would last for hours, and that sometimes an unknown voice would be heard answering back. At first the family thought that it was their child answering himself using a different voice, it was only later that they began to believe that the doll was actually talking to their son.

It was said that Robert was often seen by neighbours moving from one window of the house to another and that many times, whilst left alone with their son, ornaments would be smashed and furniture would end up broken beyond repair. Each time the boy would be blamed yet he would insist that it was the doll that was causing all of the damage.

When Eugene died in 1974 the doll was consigned to the attic until its new owners found it and gave it to their ten-year-old daughter. Time and again they were awoken by her screams of terror. Each time she would tell the same story about how the doll was moving around the room and wanted to kill her.

Robert now resides in a museum and art gallery located in Key West, though visitors are advised that if they wish to take a picture of the doll, it would be wise to ask his permission first, as many former visitors have fallen upon torrid times after stealing a quick snap of him without asking first. Letters asking for his permission post-photograph adorn the  wall nearest his display case. (True Tales of Haunted Dolls, 2013.)

However terrifying those examples may seem, when it comes to spiritual attachment this is the exception and not the norm. It is at this point that I would like to introduce Jayne Harris, founder of Haunted Dolls Paranormal Research and expert in spiritual attachment. It is her vast experiences that we shall spend the bulk of this book discussing.

Introducing Jayne Harris

Jayne's curiosity with all things paranormal started at a very young age.

"I remember as a child hearing my parents telling their friends about experiences that they had had. Seeing ghosts, hearing things, that sort of thing. My parents were both very strong believers in the paranormal, and my father's grandmother had practised as a medium. My interest was sparked further when in the year 2000 aged 17, I lost my cousin. She was like my sister, we did everything together, but at 16 she was killed in a car accident. It was then that I really began searching for answers. I felt desperation for a long time to reach out and really 'touch' the other side."

It was then that Jayne started to attend a spiritualist church in her hometown of Stratford upon Avon.

"In all honesty, I never really experienced anything that for me offered concrete proof of an afterlife. Then one day I heard a lady in the congregation telling her friend about a doll she owned that was apparently haunted. I couldn't help but listen in on their conversation, I was so fascinated, and I turned around and asked her if that what she was saying was really true? She looked at me a bit strangely and said, 'Of course it's true, love.' She carried on talking and I was absolutely gobsmacked by some of the things she described. Part of me at the time did think that she must be some kind of nutcase if I am honest, but a deeper part of me wondered as to the possibilities."

Her interest piqued, Jayne began her research in earnest.

"At that time you didn't just jump onto a computer and start researching things, so I started looking in various bookshops around

the area specifically for books that discussed the paranormal. I would scan the indexes looking for anything that seemed to relate to spirit attachment (I admit that I was actually looking for anything relating to the term 'possessed' at that time as I didn't really understand what spirit attachment actually compromised of), but most of the time I drew a blank.

"I kept attending the church, mindful to always say hello to the lady who claimed to have a haunted doll. Then one evening, I asked her if she had ever shown the doll to anyone. She said that she hadn't as everyone she had told about the doll either thought she was crazy or were too scared to visit. I told her that I would love to see it and she agreed to show me. A few days later I paid her a visit. She did not live too far from my home and I spent the whole journey conjuring up grand visions of a doll that spins its head of its own accord, or one which runs around like 'Chucky' from the Child's Play movies. It makes me cringe now that I understand this kind of thing better, but at that time, aged about 18, I only really had films and TV on which to base my assumptions.

"That evening remains as fresh in my mind as if it only occurred last night. I sat on her 1960s velour sofa with a cup of tea on my lap and my mouth WIDE open. She began by asking me if I would mind introducing myself first to 'Chrissy' (this was the doll's name) as she could be shy of strangers. Naturally I complied. She then asked Chrissy if she was happy to have a visitor. No sooner had she finished asking the question then the television flicked itself on. Not to any particular channel, just the grainy 'snowstorm' effect that you see when the channel is not tuned in correctly. As quickly as it came on, it went off again and I was told that Chrissy was here.

"I visited the lady a handful of times over the course of about six months, and far from being scared or apprehensive, I found it comforting to know or at least believe that I now had found proof that something more existed once we leave our earthly bodies behind. I started to grow in confidence when talking about the paranormal and the spirit world as time went on, and the more *people I spoke to, the more I learnt. On a personal level I also knew deep down that this was the world that I wanted to be part of. Growing up I had always wanted to become a doctor, but at 15 my life took a slightly different path (as is so often the case), and so that plan was lost. I like to think that maybe that had all happened for a reason and that at age 18 I had finally found my true calling."*

A Bespoke Service – 'Haunted Dolls'

It would still be many years before the introduction of the Haunted Dolls website. Jayne continued to visit the spiritualist churches in her area and attended several shows by highly respected mediums such as Colin Fry and Tony Stockwell. As Jayne's collection of paranormal literature began to expand so did her knowledge and it was not long before a concerned home owner contacted Jayne to ask for her help and expertise.

> *"After being asked in 2002 by someone to go and see what I thought about things they were experiencing at their home, word soon spread that I knew a bit about this kind of thing and I had several people ask me to 'investigate' their home. I've never charged anyone, as they were kind of doing me a favour in helping me study and learn more."*

Jayne's interest in all things paranormal continued to go from strength to strength, and over the course of the next few years she began to amass a large collection of dolls and curios that reputedly held connections to the spirit world.

> *"I actually got to the stage where I couldn't have friends over to my house as they were a bit uncomfortable with the amount of objects, dolls, equipment and things I had in the house. You couldn't see the dining table for files and paperwork!"*

In order to continue her investigation into spiritual attachment she came to the conclusion that she would have to move some of her collection on in order to make way for fresh items in which she could devote her time. The foundations for Haunted Dolls were set.

"I set up my website in 2012 and at that time it was just a personal blog type site where I would document my own photographs and experiences. Then I got to the point where I had used up both of my spare rooms housing dolls and other curiosities...

"...So I offered a couple of my own dolls up on the website. I knew what I had paid for them, and I worked out how many hours roughly I had spent researching them in order to gain detailed information. This was how I decided on a price and that model stays the same today. The more documented hours of study time, the more travel and preparation we have to do, and the more we have to pay for a study piece initially, dictates its cost to a collector later on. This allows us to continue to travel, purchase further items to research and so goes the cycle. We're not out to make huge profits. As long as we can keep doing what we love."

In the early days of Jayne's investigations she would often be accompanied by her husband and a couple of friends who shared her enthusiasm for all things paranormal. This was the case until recently when the couple moved away from the area. Jayne's husband still helps with the investigative side of the business from time to time, but the bulk of the work largely rests upon Jayne's shoulders.

Having established herself as one of the leading lights in the field of spiritual attachment (she is officially endorsed by the British Paranormal Association), it may not surprise you to hear that her client list is both large and varied.

"Our clients can be anyone. We have had doctors, teachers, students, artists, an ex-FBI agent, a puppeteer you name it! Spirits are not choosy about who they get to know! The one thing all collectors obviously have in common is an interest in the paranormal."

Whilst word of mouth and endorsements are key to building a successful business and a solid reputation, it is the advent of social media that has really enabled Jayne to engage with her clients and helped her to push her ethos further than she had dare to imagine.

As mentioned earlier, Haunted Dolls recently received an official endorsement from the British Paranormal Association (http://www.britishparanormal.org.uk), an honour that Jayne is rightly proud of. Paranormal investigations have become huge business over the last few years and an endorsement from the BPA guarantees potential customers that they will be dealing with both a professional and knowledgeable individual.

"The BPA (British Paranormal Association) was set up by various leaders in their field of the paranormal. It's a non-profit organisation that basically works to share best practise and so forth. Their website includes a section for 'rogue companies' amongst other things so they basically work to promote 'legit' organisations."

Her work has also caught the attention of *Paranormal Magazine*. (www.paranormalunderground.net) who wrote a feature article on a doll named Matilda that Jayne had offered as a competition prize. (The website often runs similar competitions, which enable visitors in the site to enter a raffle where the prize is one of the dolls from Jayne's personal collection.)

"There was a five page article in Paranormal Underground *magazine giving a case study of one of our dolls, Matilda. A guy from the magazine won one of our competitions but didn't tell us who he was! We sent him the doll and he studied her and reported his findings."*

Haunted Dolls was also referenced by *Living Dead Magazine* in an article titled 'Haunted Objects – Fact or Fiction?' (www.living deadmagazine.com)

You can find out more about Jayne's business on Facebook by searching for **Haunted Dolls** or by visiting www.haunted-dolls.com.

New customers are always welcome and are exceptionally well catered for. All dolls and curios come complete with an extensive history and Jayne offers advice and support that is personally tailored to the needs of each object and its prospective owner.

What is Spirit Attachment?

If one were to research the topic of spirit attachment you would find that the vast majority of recorded cases relate to the attachment of a spirit upon an individual. Indeed, instances wherein energy attaches itself to an object seem far rarer by comparison. In order to answer why this is the case it is first necessary to examine what happens when a spirit attaches itself to a person.

It is only in recent times that the concept of a spirit attachment has caught the interest of the public. Novels such as *The Exorcist* by William Peter Blatty (and the subsequent movie), have infiltrated mainstream horror and portray the more severe form of spirit attachment (possession), but it is important to note that there are distinctive differences between the two phenomena.

Spirit attachment occurs when the energy or spirit from a deceased person 'latches' onto a living person. (Paranormal Experiences – What is Spirit Attachment, 2012.) The relationship between the living host and the deceased spirit is one of a parasitic nature. It is argued that the spirit 'leeches' from the living in order to sustain itself. This draining effect can cause many unpleasant side effects, but most cases of spirit attachment largely go unnoticed by sufferers of the phenomena due to their apparent similarities with established physical and psychological conditions. (Peter Michael, 2007.)

It may well be that cases of human spirit attachment appear far more prevalent than those that ground themselves to objects as it is easier for a spirit to attach to a 'live' host. It is argued that spirits seek out living souls as a means of comfort. The deceased may find death hard to accept and therefore seek to remain earthbound in order to continue to experience life and its many pleasures. It is also suggested that some return to the earthly plane in order to attach to those with whom the deceased share a particular trait or talent. (Peter Michael, 2007.) Other spirits may wish to make contact with the living in order to pass on a message that they did not have the chance to pass on in life.

The list of explanations and arguments are numerous and varied when it comes to discussing this particular form of attachment, and it is likely that the debates will continue to rage until we receive some form of concrete proof regarding the existence of spirits and the afterlife. However, for the purpose of this book, we shall explore the types of attachment that occur when a spirit forgoes the prospect of attachment with a living host and chooses to anchor itself to an inanimate object. (Paranormal Experiences – What is Spirit Attachment, 2012.)

How Does a Spirit
Attach Itself to an Object?

Dave Schumacher is the Director of the Anomalous Research Department of the Pennsylvania and Wisconsin based *Paranormal Research Group*, and he suggests that there are three key theories that may explain how and why a spirit attaches itself to an object. (Haunted Objects, Robin M. Strom-Mackey 2012.)

Theory One: The Residual Haunt

The residual haunt theory suggests that certain events can be so emotionally charged that they can end up leaving an imprint on the surrounding environment. Any object or building close to the event has the potential to store the energy that is released, holding it until a time where certain environmental conditions occur and a playback of the event is triggered. Playback may include auditory phenomena (such as the sound of someone crying), or visual apparitions. This playback is non-interactive and remains constant (in that repeated playbacks all feature exactly the same activity). This is similar to the stone tape theory mentioned earlier in that if a building or a location is able to store such energy then maybe singular items are also able to do the same.

The ability to read the 'history' of an object is known as psychometry. This ability allows a medium to read the history of an object merely by touch. It is argued that actual contact with a spirit that is grounded to such an item is extremely limited and that the medium is able to see the history of an object through a series of images.

Psychic medium and psychometrist, Pat Patalona (*Balzano*, Weisberg, 2012) states that she often sees different episodes in the history of an object, though one may be more emotionally charged than another. For instance she may pick up only one person attached to an object despite the fact that the object had numerous owners.

She explains the recording process thus: "Everything in the universe has an energy field that radiates all around it. These emotions, these impressions, they are absorbed with that energy field. It's not necessarily inside the object, but it exists in that energy field. I read that energy." (*Balzano*, Weisberg, 2012).

It is widely believed amongst mediums that objects made of gold in particular [also known for its electrical conductivity] tends to hold onto the greatest amount of energy. (Haunted Objects, Robin M. Strom-Mackey 2012.)

Theory 2: Retro-cognition

This is the ability to perceive or relive experiences that occurred in the past usually via the form of a vision or a dream. These visions tend to be vivid and include elements of sights, sounds and smells. Those gifted in this sense have described the process similar to stepping into that time for short a period. An object may hold the memory of a past event, and in the hands of someone with the ability to read it, play back those memories or stored energies. It is suggested that all hauntings are retro-cognitive events where the past scene is read telepathically in the present. (Cheung, 2006.)

Theory Three: The Intelligent Haunt

The intelligent haunt theory suggests that part of the human consciousness survives the body after death. The consciousness released from the body may return to a location or an object that it felt a strong connection with during life. Thus if someone were attached to a particular possession in life they might indeed return to it after death. (Haunted Objects, Robin M. Strom-Mackey 2012.)

The Difference between Attachment and Possession

It is important to point out now that experts in the field of spiritual attachment draw a clear and distinctive line between the phenomena of 'attachment' and 'possession'.

Jayne explains why it is believed that an object cannot be possessed.

"There is a clear distinction between 'spirit possession' and 'spirit attachment'. Most cases found on attachment are relating to people not objects; however, these cases are actually spirit possession. This is when a spirit will quite literally 'possess' the shell, but not the soul of a human being as a means to an end. Many believe that 'end' to be ultimately taking ownership of the person's soul.

"Spirit attachment that involves an object relates more in terms of residual energy with elements of individual intelligence remaining after life has expired. Elements of someone's soul anchor themselves to an inanimate object as a way of remaining on the earthly plane. We believe that as all things are made up of matter and energy, that by anchoring one's own energy (which some believe would otherwise be in 'limbo') to a specific object, spirits create for themselves a doorway or portal. Through this physical object they can return here or remain here.

"In cases of Spirit Possession individuals are largely dealing with a darker force. There are usually unhuman elements at play."
(Jayne Harris, 2014)

Parapsychologists believe that Psychology also plays a key part in a vast amount of suspected attachment cases.

"There are also a few psychological possibilities for haunted objects as well. Dave Schumacher suggests magical thinking, sheer human

imagination, and the desire to experience a paranormal event, subjective validation and confirmation bias. In other words, if a person is inclined toward believing in the paranormal they're more likely to attribute unexplained phenomenon to being paranormal." (Haunted Objects, Robin M. Strom-Mackey 2012.)

Spirit Attachment throughout History

Belief in spirit attachment is by no means restricted to those cultures that are built upon the foundations of Christianity. Japanese folklore believes that once an object reaches 100 years of age it receives a soul (Tsukumogami). Known examples have included a possessed mirror (Ugaikyo) and a possessed clock (Zorigami). There is even a ceremony called Jinja that *consoles and comforts* objects which have been broken or thrown away.

The concept of spirited items is widely accepted in the religion of Voodoo. For example twins are considered sacred by practitioners for they believe that the two individuals carry two halves of the same soul. Should one of them pass away it is quite common for the surviving twin to carry a doll that resembles their deceased sibling. The belief is that the doll harbours the other half of the soul, and that by carrying the doll the soul remains intact.

Voodoo also has a notoriously dark side to the religion and there is a strong belief that witchdoctors are able to bind souls against their will to an item after death through the use of black magic and blood rituals.

In China, travelling puppeteers often transported their puppets with the characters head kept separate from the body. The idea was that by doing this, any bad spirits that may have inhabited the doll would not be able to take full possession of the doll and cause trouble. A separated vessel meant that the spirit would not be able to exert its full hold over the puppet.

Countless more theories and beliefs can be found throughout history of cultures that subscribe to the idea of spirit attachment in one form or another. This book hopes to give the reader a very basic overview of some of the more modern theories behind these beliefs.

Investigative Methods and Tools

When it comes to investigating an item that potentially has a spirit attached to it, Jayne approaches this in two ways. Jayne will either visit the item and the owner at their place of residence or speak to them intensively over the telephone. It is here that she will make copious notes that cover the background history of the object (how and when it came into the owners possession), and will ask questions about any unusual events that have occurred in the house or around the object that may indicate the belief that paranormal activity is taking place. Often the owners of the item will report cold spots or unusual sounds emanating from rooms that are known to be unoccupied (such as tapping or hurried footsteps). The purpose of this conversation is to gather as much background information as possible and to rule out anything in the environment that could be causing the phenomena that the client believes to be paranormal.

Like most of her peers, Jayne uses a selection of equipment and techniques to help her in her initial investigation and she will usually bring these with her when she meets a client. She is sure to always carry her K2 meter, a pendulum (made from onyx), an object or charm that is personal to her (in order that she feels grounded and safe from harm), and a digital camera.

Of course technology is no substitute for intuition as Jayne explains:

> *"As a general guide, if I feel from what someone has told me over the phone that a visit would benefit further from feedback on an intuitive level, I will ask for the company of our regular psychic medium Hazel (and prior to Hazel a lady named Kathleen) whose presence can prove invaluable. Throughout my research studies, the knowledge and information she can provide through mediumship often guides me in the approach I subsequently take."*

Haunted Dolls Investigation Equipment
Pictured: Headphones, Infrared Camera, K2 Meter, Onyx Pendulum, Mini Digital Recorder, Dowsing rods, Trip Sensor, Charm Bag, EMF Camera.

K2 Meter

The K2 meter (Jayne uses one produced by Ovilus,) is a portable electromagnetic field (EMF) detection unit. When it detects the presence of a magnetic field, internal circuitry is activated and the device shows the strength of the detected field via a series of LEDs. The more of these that light up, the stronger the detected magnetic field. (How Does a K2 Meter Work, Andy Pasquesi, 2014.)

The Paranormal community believe that spirits can produce and manipulate magnetic fields. Therefore they are often used as a means to test a spirits reaction to questions posed by an investigator. The theory behind this is that a strong reading on the K2 meter when corresponding to a question asked about the spirit is taken to indicate a positive response by the spirit.

Parapsychologists argue that electromagnetic fields can also influence the people that are captured within them. The sensations people report that they experience and feel are very similar in nature to those of a suspected haunting.

Michael Persinger, Professor of Psychology at Laurentian University, Ontario, Canada, has a theory regarding EMF. His theory, which he presents in a chapter in the book *Hauntings and Poltergeists* (McFarland & Co, 2001), is that the sensation commonly described as "having a paranormal experience" is merely a side effect of both sides of our brain trying to work together. Simplified, the idea goes like this: When the right hemisphere of the brain, the side associated with emotion, is stimulated in a particular part of the cerebral region, and then the left hemisphere, the language side, is called upon to make sense of these stimulations, the mind generates a "sense of presence." Dr. Persinger believes such cerebral "fritzing" is responsible for almost anything we might describe as paranormal such as apparitions, ghost lights, poltergeist activity, and so on. Experimental subjects who were exposed to a specific series of pulses from TMS (transcranial magnetic stimulation) described feeling an invisible presence near them or feeling connected to the whole world. (West Norfolk Paranormal, ND.)

The key to using a tool well is to understand how it works, and the same can be said of the K2 meter. Whenever you investigate a new property (or unpack your own K2 meter in your own home) it is important to use the device to explore your surroundings in order to gain a feel for the amount of electromagnetic activity that is naturally occurring. This is known as a set of baseline measurements, and recording and understanding these are vital before you begin to try to find evidence of paranormal activity. Once you know the 'normal' operating range of the electromagnetic fields produced in your surroundings you will easily be able to spot any later anomalies. For example, a standard reading on a K2 meter taken from any light fitting or appliance, can range from anywhere between 0.1 and 10 mG (milliGauss). If you are testing an area near to a typical domestic appliance such as a washing machine or television you can expect to see readings around the 30 mG mark. If you are ever in doubt as to whether an appliance is producing more of an EMF reading than it should, you can consult the manual that the appliance came with and check what the manufacturer has recorded as its usual EMF output. (West Norfolk Paranormal, ND.)

It is also important to note that when using a K2 meter and a spike of activity is detected (this is where the LEDs light up suggesting you have hit upon a EMF somewhere in the vicinity), it is important to stand still. Even the slightest movement can cause the reading to fluctuate and give a 'muddy' measurement. (West Norfolk Paranormal, ND.)

K2 meters are extremely sensitive pieces of equipment and respond to mobile phones, wireless microphones, broadband, Wi-Fi and walkie-talkies. It is important to remember this fact when conducting an investigation where accurate readings are a necessity. (Ghost Hunting 101: what is a K-II meter and how do I use it?)

There are many 'fake' K2 meters for sale due to the huge surge in popularity of ghost hunting so it is in the consumer's interest to be careful when they purchase one. According to Jayne, *"Genuine K2 meters have a matt finish whereas Fake K2s have a gloss finish. Genuine K2s have a protective sponge circle inside protecting the motherboard whereas the Fake K2 has nothing. Both come with identical instruction manuals."*

Pendulum

The pendulum is another popular tool used by paranormal investigators. Its application is simple and almost anything that hangs by a thread, chain or wire can be used as a pendulum, though most practitioners of this form use a dedicated crystal.

For example Jayne uses a 'snowflake obsidian'. She explains that *"I was once told that you should choose to use the stone you are drawn the most to, and mine just happened to be obsidian."*

The pendulum is used to determine the yes or no answer to a question that is asked of the spirit. For example, the investigator may dictate that if the pendulum rotates clockwise that would indicate a positive response – if anti clockwise that would indicate a negative response. It is also possible to gather numerical information from a spirit using the pendulum technique. One could ask the spirit to indicate his or her age when they passed over by swinging the pendulum in either direction the relevant amount of times. (Malkuths Ghost – How to use a pendulum, 2009.)

Pendulums are relatively simple to use though some practitioners achieve better results than others do.

Some people are naturally gifted at pendulum use. This seems to have no connection with whether they're believers or sceptics. Some people can use pendulums, but they internalize the energy. That's not a good idea. *If you can't remain* completely separate *from the pendulum you're using, stop immediately. Do* not *allow outside energy to be channelled through your body to the pendulum. (And, if you can't tell the difference, don't use a pendulum. The risks are too great.)* (Ghosts 101, Fiona Broom, 2009.)

Critics of the technique cite that the results obtained by using a pendulum can be corrupted by the user's unconscious movements. John Fraser states in his Ghost Hunting: A Survivor's Guide (2010) that

...at worst, movements are caused by no more than unconscious muscular action by anyone holding the rod or pendulum, interpreted as signals from the beyond, a view encouraged by the organisers of events who are either principally concerned with entertainment,

making money, or confirming pre-existing beliefs. At best –
assuming some dowsing ability is operating – twitches by the rod or
swings of the pendulum are still being generated by muscular
actions, as a subconscious reaction to any manner of things present.
(*Fourtean Times*, 'Ghost Hunters and the Delights of Dowsing',
Alan Murdie, 2012.)

Like the K2 meter, it is suggested that before engaging with a
spirit you should collect a few baseline readings regarding your
surroundings. These are attained by simply letting the
pendulum hang and noting any movements that may be caused
by airflow or by standing on an uneven floor and so forth.

Charms

The choice of carrying charms or crystals is deeply personal.
With the abundance of crystals available, each of which has their
own unique characteristics and benefits, it would be impossible
to discuss all of their merits within this book. Concentrating on
Jayne's choices, she chooses to carry rose quartz and angel hair
quartz stating that they are great for purity and attracting
positive energies. Other items she carries with her include a
small horseshoe (believed to be lucky and given to her by her
grandmother), a leather bracelet that belonged to her cousin
(who was her reason for her interest in the paranormal in the
beginning), and a 'worry doll' (although Jayne readily admits
that carrying this doll is more to do with her personal super-
stition rather that it being a necessity for an investigation.
Note on worry dolls:

The indigenous people from the Highlands in Guatemala created
Worry Dolls many generations ago as a remedy for worrying.
According to the Mayan legend, when worrying keeps a person
awake, he or she tells a worry to as many dolls as necessary. Then
the worrier places the dolls under his or her pillow. The dolls take

over the worrying for the person who then sleeps peacefully through the night. When morning breaks, the person awakens without the worries that the dolls took away during the night. (The Worry Depository, Sara Mcdonell, 2008.)

Camera

With the array of affordable technology available today a digital camera is a must. Cameras often capture things unseen by the naked eye, and though most can be easily explained via careful examination, some are not. However, as Jayne describes below, even a smartphone camera can be used to capture images of paranormal activity. *"Our camera is a Canon SLR, but I must confess to using my smartphone (Samsung Galaxy S5) just as much to capture things as I always have it in my pocket. Sometimes it's much quicker to grab."*

Advanced Investigative
Techniques and Equipment

The second part of the investigation is conducted back at Jayne's residence. The object in question is brought back to be looked at in greater detail. Usually this follows the home visit as detailed earlier, but occasionally people do send her things to investigate based on the strength of her reputation.

Upon arrival the object is transferred to the lower section of the basement. This is the area that Jayne has set up for dedicated investigative practice. Situated there is the glass isolation cabinet where every item that is brought into the house will spend the first 24 hours. The cabinet is surrounded by salt and a set of rosary beads reside on the top. (It has long been believed that amongst its many properties salt has the ability to absorb vast

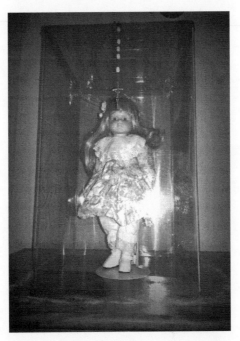

Pictured: The Isolation Cabinet with a doll in situ.

amounts of psychic energy. Magical properties of Salt, NA, ND.) The cabinet was originally a gift to Jayne and forms an integral part of her studies. It has been blessed and is anointed with holy water every six months.

Once the object is set inside the cabinet, a series of photographs are taken to record the position of the item. A night vision camera is set to record the object throughout the night alongside a digital sensor. Occasionally, trigger objects are added into the cabinet alongside the object to be studied. Jayne will alter the trigger item depending upon the history of the object. For example, if Jayne receives a doll that allegedly has the spirit of a small child attached to it she may leave a toy alongside the doll in the hopes of encouraging some form of paranormal inter-action. Again, all of the positions of the objects that are left are marked and recorded using a camera.

A digital recorder is also set up to capture any instances of electronic voice phenomena (EVP.) EVP occurs when human-sounding voices from an unknown source are heard on a form of recording. The voices are not heard at the time of recording; it is only when the tape is played back that the voices are heard although sometimes amplification and noise filtering is required to hear the voices.

EVP usually takes the form of spoken single words, and phrases or short sentences (or both). Occasionally they can be groans, growls or sobs. EVP has been recorded speaking in various languages. (All you need to know about Electronic Voice Phenomena, Stephen Wagner, ND.)

Jayne and her team are careful to note any occurrences whilst the item is confined to observation. These have often included sudden temperature changes, unexplained noises, atmospheric changes, odd shadows or orb sightings. All of these incidents are typed up and recorded alongside the findings from the initial investigation to create a dedicated file for each item that comes into Jayne's care.

Once the 24-hour window has elapsed further photographs are taken and a comparison is made with those that were taken at the beginning of the items isolation. It is here that any movements are noted.

This isolation period is repeated several times over the following few months and all recorded data is analysed by Jayne and her team. They look for patterns of repeated behaviour for which they are unable to find an explanation. This is how they define whether an item has a genuine attachment. These preliminary findings dictate how the team proceed with the item in future.

Pictured: Close up of isolated doll

Cleansing

In cases where an object brought into the house reputedly has a dark energy attached to it a cleansing ritual is required.

"Cleansing is very important. If we feel that we have a spirited doll that has a dark energy associated with it or feel that the spirit has retreated or is in some way unsettled, it is then that we conduct a cleansing ritual.

"We take the object or the doll along with a white candle, salt, sage, lavender, a bowl of water and a piece of jade (or quartz for fabric-bodied dolls). When using a doll we strip it of any clothing and accessories. Obviously if it has clothing that is stitched to the body or items that cannot easily be removed then it's fine to leave

Pictured: A doll prepared for a cleansing ritual.

these on. A doll that can be fully stripped of all fabric (usually plastic dolls) should be placed in water containing sage and a cross should also be marked on the chest (again using sage)."

(Sage has long been believed to help ward off dark or evil spirits and used as a cleansing agent by many different cultures – 'Benefits and Uses of White Sage', Amanda Linette Meder, ND.)

"A doll that has a fabric body (usually a porcelain doll) should simply have a sage cross marked onto its chest and a piece of jade or quartz placed on the head. The quartz and the water act as a reflector for positivity. A circle of salt is formed around the doll or object in order to absorb any negative energy that may leak from the object into the atmosphere of the home.

"Once all is ready, I sit in front of the item for a few minutes and clear my mind of any negative thoughts or emotions. When I feel ready to begin I repeat the words, 'Be cleansed with light, Be cleansed with light' until I feel I have made a connection with the entity that is attached to the object before me. This usually takes about six or seven attempts. I then hold my hands above the doll, careful to make sure that I do not make any physical contact.

"I then imagine the negativity contained within the object as a black mist being drawn up through the item and into my hands (some people report actually seeing this physically although I have not as yet).

"I then visualise a pure bright white light surrounding the item, which it then absorbs. This is how I see the negativity being nullified in my mind.

"When the ritual is complete I blow out the candle and wave my hands through the candle smoke to remove any trace of negative energy from my hands. The item is then left in a state of isolation overnight."

Jayne's basement workspace.

Case Studies

Jayne has investigated countless dolls and curiosities from all over the world, yet sometimes the stories attached to the piece in question are so bizarre and the paranormal activity associated with them so intense that they leave an indelible imprint upon her. It is now that she presents some of her favourite, spooky or downright weird case studies. They are drawn from her personal archives and are presented to you in her own words.

PETER: A vintage rag doll – large with painted features.

Peter
Origin: Amsterdam, Holland.
Joined us: October 2012.
Known Spirit: A young boy aged 12 named Peter.
Activity displayed: Loud bangs created either by things either falling or being knocked over. Other noises were

unexplainable. Doors would bang, orbs would frequently be seen as a grey mist, which would appear and disappear at will. Peter would also appear in dreams. His doll incited high K2 readings.

During a visit to Amsterdam in 2012, I had heard whisperings while I was there about a strange doll that was on display at the Noordermarkt flea market. Apparently the doll was making things fall from the table he was sitting on. This happened each week and the stallholder was convinced it was the doll (which was nameless at the time). Of course I had to see this, so I went one Saturday morning and sure enough, there was Peter, sitting on a table surrounded by items like shoes, tins, horseshoes and so on. As I continued around the market I found that I couldn't take my eyes off him. He seemed to watch me the whole time I was there. When I finally got around to his table, I asked if he was for sale. The stallholder said that he was, but was guarding the place for him at the moment. I found this so amusing. He looked like a naughty little boy about to steal something rather than someone to trust with his stall. We chatted for a while and in the end the stallholder asked me to come back to see him when the market was closing and he would talk to me more about the doll (he insisted that there were things I should know about the doll).

Intrigued, I went for a stroll and came back around 1pm. When I arrived back at the stall I found that most things were packed away except the doll and a few pieces of furniture. Peter was sitting on an old antique chair and I remember thinking that he seemed almost curious of me – almost as though he wondered why I was back and what I was doing. The stallholder suggested we go for a coffee and he would tell me all about the doll. So I accompanied Jan (who had by this point introduced himself) to a local cafe. It was there that he told us about how he couldn't take the doll home as his wife would not have it in the house. She feared it greatly and she was sure that there was a "devil inside it". (I'll take this opportunity to assure you that I have since made contact with the spirit associated with the doll, and he is not a dark energy or anything to be feared.)

Jan explained why his wife was so uncomfortable with the doll. He spoke of doors banging in their home when his wife was alone with the doll and that she felt as though she was being watched. She even went so far as to remove move him out of the bedroom or would take to covering his face when she was getting dressed!

Week after week Jan promised his wife that he would sell the doll at the market but nobody seemed to want him. This week was to be his last attempt at selling the doll. Failure to do so would mean he was to throw the doll away. I was so relieved, and almost felt a sense that I was meant to find him that day, and immediately made an offer for him. I knew I wanted to know more about him as I was convinced by this point that there was indeed a spirit attached to the doll.

Peter came home with us and I took him to see my friend (and psychic medium) Kathleen. At first she couldn't connect (which is unusual and I did worry that I had made a mistake). However, after a few attempts without using a communication tool (instead choosing to speak aloud to him) the spirit of Peter came through. He explained that he was a shy boy who liked to play tricks and hide. Over an initial study period of 10 days (mainly through the use of a pendulum and Kathleen's dream diaries) we established the following information:

Peter was British. He had been on holiday in Amsterdam in 1978 when he was 12, when his father bought him the doll. He loved it, and named him after himself. Peter had tragically drowned when he slipped into a river during a boat trip. He was leaning over the side and went over. He went straight under the boat and couldn't find his way back up. He recalled feeling very cold and that he couldn't breathe before suddenly feeling very warm and happy. He had such a strong bond with the doll that he said he had wanted to stay with him.

We asked Peter if he wanted to be sent across to the other side, and he did not. He said he didn't know what was over there so he wanted to stay. We respected his wishes and are really pleased he decided to stay. Since owning Peter, I too have experienced the banging of doors, and items falling from shelves and so on. Peter seems to like to play with books and I often find several of my books on the floor next to the bookcase as if someone has been pulling them down.

The K2 meter often picks up energy around him too (which coincides with a variety of expected behaviour from him), and as captured in one of his photographs, a white-grey mist can also be seen, usually when Peter is at his most active.

Pictured: Peter (with the unexplained 'mist' that is sometimes seen around him).

Helen Emily Greyford
Large porcelain doll circa 1970 with soft body.
Origin: Mid Wales, UK.

Joined us: May 2013.

Known Spirit: A young girl aged 17 named Helen. Died in the early part of the 1800s. She was accused of theft and hung.

Activity displayed during investigations: Pendulums are incredibly active. Numerous Orbs, occasional shadowy figure in photographs around her. Doll's facial changes are frequently witnessed. Sudden and unexplainable cold rushes of air are felt around her. Helen also communicates during séances.

Pictured: Helen

Helen came into our possession after we were called to investigate a small terraced house in mid Wales. She was found by the owner in the old shed at the bottom of his garden.

Her new owners instantly felt uncomfortable around her as Helen does have a strong presence about her (one that we couldn't deny the moment we saw her!). They had no evidence she was attached to the spirit world but they suspected as much.

We noted the heavy atmosphere in the home upon entering. K2 readings were intermittent, but registered consistently high when discussing the doll.

We conducted several experiments with Helen including several group séances, which were held by our psychic professional Kathleen. This is how we discovered Helen's fate.

Helen and her brother Adam had gone into the village looking for food to purchase. They didn't have a great deal of money but they were from an honest, hardworking family. Whilst bartering for various items a lady began shouting at Helen and accused her of being a thief. Helen had never stolen anything in her life (upon the retelling of this story, Kathleen became extremely emotional – as did the rest of us in attendance). Helen was chased as far as the local authorities building by which time she had lost sight of Adam. In her hand, Helen held a small piece of bread that she had been intending to pay for, but in the panic she had simply ran. This sealed her fate. She was held in a small cell for two days, after which she was publicly executed for theft.

We feel that Helen is desperate to clear her name although she has never revealed the name of the place she lived. We know it was southern England but we cannot be sure. Maybe this will come to light in time.

The images below were captured during investigative work. The two images we taken one after the other. You can see a figure in the background of the second image that we didn't notice at the time. This was taken following a very active investigation conducted on The Devils Chair in Shropshire.

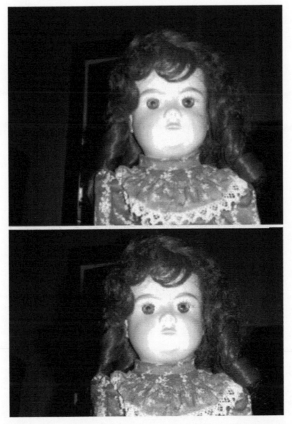

**Pictured: Helen with an unexplained shadow appearing in the
second shot that was not seen at the time of the image being taken
(seen left of doll).**

Helen likes to be the centre of attention, and we feel this is why
the pendulum work is very successful with her. During our
investigation on The Devils Chair, Helen fell from a rock while
we were questioning another spirit. Her little finger was broken,
and although we found it beneath the second doll, it has since
disappeared.

Pictured: Image of Helen taken via a night vision camera.

Pearl

Origin: Tamworth, UK (Pearl lived in Aberystwyth).

Joined us: May 2006.

Known Spirit: A woman in her 60s named Pearl (although her apparition manifests as a woman in her 30s as this was Pearl's happiest time.)

Activity displayed during investigations: Sudden and powerful smell of warm bread, the outdoors and fresh clean linen. Soft singing can often heard around 11pm. Very cold rushes of air. A feeling of being watched when she is in the room. Pearl has appeared several times to our group. The wheels of the little elephant the doll carries have been heard squeaking in the night.

We were called to the residence of the Sollar's family in Tamworth. They had purchased a large porcelain doll from an antique fair for their daughter but were becoming increasingly concerned, as their daughter (who was aged five at the time) was becoming obsessed with having long conversations with the doll, and often wouldn't even leave her bedroom for meals! They had heard from a neighbour about the work we do and they decided to see if anything was going on with the doll.

When we arrived we all commented on how warm and homely the place was and how we didn't feel the presence of any negativity or heavy energy at all. Admittedly, I thought this sure to be a case of non-paranormal activity. The family had arranged for their daughter to be at a friend's house when we arrived, so we used the K2 and pendulum alone in the little girl's bedroom.

At first we found nothing. Then, 23 minutes into the session the K2 shot up to a high 'RED' reading. We moved around the room wondering if there was any electrical interference present but the reading was only high when placed upon the doll. We decided to push ahead and began questioning the doll. The pendulum swung furiously but no definite answers were given.

Our curiosity was raised enough for us to suggest to the parents that they let us study her further. They were relieved to be rid of her

Once Home

Over the course of 11 months (largely through use of the pendulum but also through group séance sessions and 121 studies) we have discovered the following:

Pearl had a granddaughter named Lily for whom she bought this exquisite doll. Lily adored the doll and sang to her all of the time. Pearl taught her a few little tunes too.

Sadly, when Lily was 10, her grandmother Pearl passed away after a short period of ill health. Pearl now tells us it was lung cancer. Lily was devastated. However, her grandmother had always told her to believe in fairies and magic and that if she could ever find a way to come back to her, she would. Pearl had no fear when it came to death for she had a plan. She had been doing a lot of research on spirit attachment and had decided when she became very ill, that if there was any way that was possible, she would remain in our world. She chose her granddaughter's beloved doll as her means of doing this.

Pearl told us that roughly six months after her passing, and after travelling through various stages of 'limbo', she found herself back in Wales, wandering the streets back towards her home. She then somehow (and she tells us she isn't sure how this happened) found herself in her granddaughter's bedroom, watching her from a windowsill. She knew then her soul was now attached to the doll and that her plan had worked.

Unfortunately, the story didn't end happily for Pearl. Lily never knew how Pearl watched over her each day, and as Pearl never made her presence known and did not want to confuse

Lily, she chose to take comfort in being around her instead. Then, just before Christmas 1990, Lily's parents decided they had to move to be closer to her father's work. Three weeks later they were gone and in the rush the doll had been forgotten. Pearl hoped that they would return, but they didn't. She later learnt they had been involved in a tragic motorway collision on the M5 and all had died at the scene.

We have worked with Pearl many times, establishing her reasons for wanting to remain, rather than pass over to be with her family, and she never gives us a detailed reason. She simply says, "My place is here."

Tammy Lynne
Origin: UK (South West).
Known Spirit: Lynette – originates from Glenrio, Texas, US. A young American woman who was murdered in 1970 aged only 22 by men that she knew.
Joined us: March 2007.
Activity displayed during investigations: Mainly music related activity. Radios (including digital apps) will switch on at random times or change stations of their own accord. Country music features prominently during this activity.

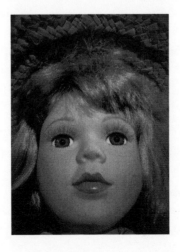

Though Lynette has spoken to our psychic several times she has never appeared to us in the form of an apparition as she states that she is ashamed of her appearance. She prefers to interact with women.

Tammy Lynne is a truly beautiful doll. She has gorgeous golden blonde curls, big blue eyes and wears a truly wonderful expression, though unfortunately the doll carries with it a sense of sadness. Lynette, the young girl connected with this doll, has experienced trauma both in life and death. Though her soul is now at peace, she has chosen to remain on this side as she told us that there are people waiting for her in the afterlife that she does not wish to associate with.

We were actually sent Tammy Lynne via post. Her owner's daughter had had enough of her mother constantly talking about "the lady in the doll". Apparently she was even afraid to sleep because of the doll!

To protect their identities for the purpose of this book, all names have been changed.

Donna emailed us during January 2007 to ask as to whether we would take a doll from her. She insisted that she would only send it to us if we promised not to contact them again and agreed to keep hold of the doll. Intrigued, I assured her that this would indeed be the case and Tammy arrived three days later.

At first I was surprised at how pretty she was and couldn't imagine why someone would be afraid of her, even if there was indeed some kind of paranormal connection. The doll came with a note, which was folded tightly under one of her arms.

Note from the previous owner

We began attempting to forge a connection with the spirit the very next day. Our psychic medium Kathleen held the doll whilst speaking to her and instantly felt that she did not want to be held yet, so she placed her down upon our dining room table. At that exact moment there was a cold rush of air and an old country-

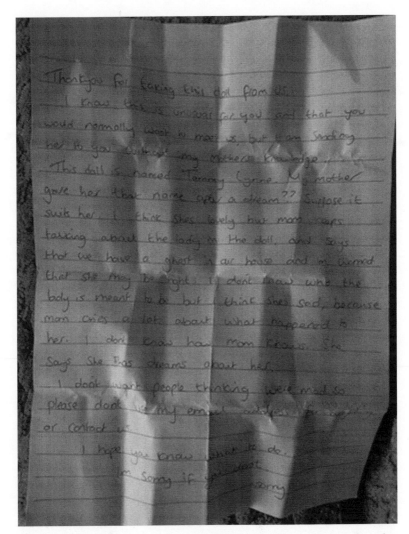

and-western song came onto the radio, which was situated in the kitchen next to us. The radio had been switched off. It was at this point that we felt another presence in the room with us.

Over the course of three months Kathleen was able to gain much information from the spirit. Tammy explained that she had died through starvation when she was only 20. She had been travelling back from a bar with her uncle and two of his friends when one of the men hit her over the head with something that felt heavy. She says she remembers a flash and a bang that occurred inside her head and then nothing until she awoke later that evening to find herself alone. The next two days passed in a blur for her, but she knows that she was sexually assaulted (or "played around with" as she puts it), before being left without food or water to die. She said that she remembers fading away very slowly.

When asked why no one had missed her or had tried to find her, she simply told us that her father had left home before she was born and that her mother was an alcoholic who never really paid her much attention. She had always being a loner with no real friends and no job. She told us the town in which she lived was called Glenrio, which was situated in Texas. When we asked if she would like to go back there she told us that there "ain't no one or nothing there for me now."

We have since done some research and found that Glenrio was once a thriving town during the time Lynette lived, as it was ideally situated upon the famous Route 66 highway. Unfortunately, when Interstate 40 was built, it signalled the end for Glenrio prosperity, as the road completely bypassed the town, taking the bulk of the passing trade with it. By 1985 there were only two residents left and it is now classed as a 'ghost town'.

Given the nature of the note that we received with Tammy Lynne, we have since contacted the previous owner's daughter (Donna) in order to verify some of the information Lynette relayed to us about the treatment of the doll at the hands of her mother. Kathleen had sensed various things that Mrs Smith had done to the doll out of fear. The spirit told her that she had thrown the doll against a wall when she had believed the doll to be watching her (hence two small marks on the face of the doll), and had bound it with tape and newspaper, before leaving it in a drawer for weeks at a time. She also threw the doll away on two occasions, only to have it bought back to her.

We had Tammy Lynne for six years and in that time we loved

her, cared for her, and showed her that the world is not a completely terrible place and that the right loving home for her does exist. In return she has provided us with many interesting experiences over the years and during our initial investigations with her we never quite knew which type of activity we would get! We have had musical interference, electrical breakdowns, orbs, cold spots and various visual phenomenon that has been associated with Tammy Lynne.

(It is worth noting that since Tammy Lynne went to a new owner in Australia, we have received updates stating her apparition has been seen in full form in their home.)

What follows is an example of what Jayne refers to as a one-to-one session. This is where she attempts to open communication with an attached spirit. The degree of success can vary significantly.

One-to-one sitting with Doll Calliope (Callie)

Present: Jayne Harris

11pm: Set up equipment for prior testing. K2 EMF meter functioning normally. Digital Audio Recorder set. Laser Grid GS1 Motion Detector Active and focused on doll. Digital Thermometer set, reading 21c.

11.30pm: Opening questions (allowing a minute or so between for responses)
"Are you here with me tonight, Callie?"
Response: Negative

"Have you felt happy today?"
Response: Mid-range flicker from Green to Yellow on EMF meter.

"I sense you're unhappy today"
Response: Mid-range flicker from Green to Yellow on EMF meter.

"Are you happy to speak with me tonight?
Response: Mid-range flicker from Green to Yellow on EMF meter.

"Would you prefer I used the pendulum?"
Response: Negative

11.40pm:
"Callie, I have been told you were born in 1936, is this correct?"
Response: HIGH range flicker from Green to Red on EMF meter.

"And is it also correct that you were 35 when you passed?"
Response: HIGH range flicker from Green to Red on EMF meter

"May I ask more about your passing?"
Response: Negative

"May I ask more about your passing?"
Response: Low range flicker from Green to Green/Yellow on EMF meter
(At this point there was a noticeable and sudden drop in temperature in the immediate area around myself and Callie.)

Thermometer now reading 17 degrees at 11.53pm
"I assume it must be difficult for you to talk about what happened to you?"
Response: Low range flicker from Green to Green/Yellow on EMF meter.

"I have been told your grandmother was involved, is that correct?"

Response: HIGH range flicker from Green to Red on EMF meter.

This willingness and desire to respond to this specific question took me by surprise as Callie had seemed reluctant to communicate strongly around the subject of her death up until this point.

"Did you die from poisoning?"

Response: Laser Grid Motion Detector signalled movement (I took several photographs at this stage; none gave any visible evidence of movement.)

"Did you die from poisoning, Callie?"

Response: Mid-range flicker from Green to Yellow on EMF meter

It was at this point I reached out and touched the doll. She felt cold on one side. I checked the walls for all possible sources of this cold air. All were relatively warm to my touch. Previous sessions held by Chris had raised the possibility that one of her arms was injured.

"Does your arm hurt, Callie?"

Response: Negative

"DID your arm hurt?"

Response: Mid-range flicker from Green to Yellow on EMF meter

12 Midnight – Pendulum & Board

"Callie, may I ask you some questions using the pendulum?"

Response: HIGH range flicker from Green to Red on EMF meter.

Using Pendulum

"Callie, is there anything specific you want to tell me before I ask anything?"
Spelt out with pendulum and board: M.E

"Me? Can you tell me what you mean?"
Spelt out with pendulum and board: M.E

"Do you feel this doll looks like you, Callie?"
Spelt out with pendulum and board: Y

I was about to ask the next question when the pendulum moved again
Spelt out with pendulum and board: H.A.I.R

"Are you unhappy with the hair?"
Spelt out with pendulum and board: Y

The hair of the doll has been dyed, or marker penned over at the front to give the appearance of black hair when in fact it is actually blonde.

"Should your hair be blonde?"
Spelt out with pendulum and board: N

"Should it be dark?"
Spelt out with pendulum and board: Y

"I'd like to ask you about your religious beliefs, Callie, is that okay?"
Spelt out with pendulum and board: Y

"Did you practice witchcraft of any kind?"

Spelt out with pendulum and board: N

Do you have any religious beliefs?
The pendulum rotated anti-clockwise for a few seconds before moving towards
Spelt out with pendulum and board: S.O.L

"Can you tell me more?"
No response.

"Can I ask you when you died, Callie?"
Spelt out with Pendulum and board: 61

"Is that 1861 or 1961?"
Spelt out with Pendulum and board: 19

"Thank you, Callie. Are you tiring?"
No response

"Shall I leave you now?"
Spelt out with pendulum and board: Y

I closed the session by thanking Callie again and saying a short blessing. Callie remained 'in situ' overnight with the motion detector active. No further movements were detected, and for the few minutes following the session the EMF meter remained inactive.

Unusual 'Secret Society' Gent's Ring
Joined us: 2007
Known Attachments: Spirited by previous owner who was a member of the Ancient Order of Druids

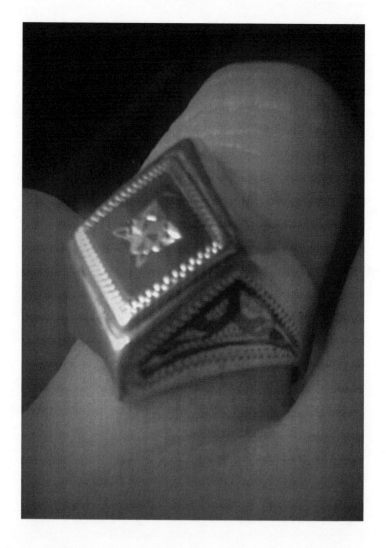

This ring came to us in 2007 from a collector of ancient druid artefacts. He had heard of our work and wondered if we had heard of his society (admittedly we hadn't). He invited me to his home is Padstow, Cornwall where I was shown a room full of fascinating articles. I had taken Hazel with me for company and it seemed it had been a wise decision to do so. We entered the house and Hazel immediately tugged on my arm and motioned towards a rocking chair that was located in the living room.

Admittedly I couldn't see anything or anyone there, but my experience told me that Hazel did.

The collector, who wished to remain anonymous hadn't really explained his reasons for calling us in any detail, except to say that he had a *visitor*. Around 45 minutes into our visit I heard a bang upstairs. It sounded much like a walking stick or a chair leg clattering upon wooden floorboards. Our host didn't seem to register the interruption and carried on chattering. As I continued to stare out of the doorway I felt as though I expected someone to walk into our meeting and my feelings of uneasiness grew. I felt sure there was something he wasn't telling us, or was building up to tell.

Suddenly Hazel asked him, "Who is the old boy upstairs then?"

Our host's expression changed immediately and he nodded in acknowledgement. He led us upstairs and into a small back bedroom which was full of a variety of collectables and druid symbolism.

He summoned both Hazel and me over to a small chest of drawers and produced the ring. Upon seeing this Hazel smiled and nodded. She believed that the ring and the apparition that she had seen in the rocking chair were linked and that this had been the cause of the 'visitations' that our host had spoken about earlier. (In addition, Hazel told me that there was a darker force also at work in the house, but as the owner was unaware or affected by this she had decided not to interfere.)

The ring belonged to a gentleman named Robert Burrows, who was for many years a member of the Ancient Order of Druids which was a secret society formed in 1781. Robert loved the ring and wore it at all times. The ring's present owner had not known Robert, but he certainly knew him once he had acquired this ring.

It has been an honour for us to own and study this ring over the past seven years. Robert's spirit is still very active around his beloved ring. We have seen Robert in our home, felt his presence, smelt his pipe and experienced the changing temperature of the ring that we were told about by its previous owner. Sometimes the ring will feel warm when worn, and then suddenly become cold. The opposite is also true. The ring is composed of sterling silver plated in gold with an unusual and intricate design around the band.

Polly (This doll was adopted by the paranormal investigation group 'Strictly Paranormal' based in Leicester. She is now a bit of a celebrity in her own right and draws in people regularly to her 'evenings with'.)

Origin: Wales, UK.

Joined us: February, 2010.

Known Spirit: A young Welsh girl called Annabelle, who died accidently in 1887 whilst playing by a stream.

Activity displayed during investigations: Light bulbs often blow in room where she is kept. Door handles rattle, pictures fall from the wall, and the sounds of children playing and giggling are often heard. Annabelle has appeared three times during our communications.

This beautiful and striking doll known as Polly came into our possession in 2010 when we were called out to investigate a farmhouse that was situated in North Wales.

The Evans family had run the farm for around 20 years and had no record of the family that had lived there previously. They were working to create a loft conversion when they came across Polly (so named by Mrs Evans,) who was wrapped in a cloth and hidden away in between the wooden beams of the roof. Mrs Evans told us that she didn't like Polly from the moment that she had found her. She said that she thought that her eyes were quite scary and that she always felt that she was being watched when the doll was around her.

Polly had been kept on a shelf in the family kitchen for a few months when things began to happen around the farm. Mr Evans was finding that things would go missing from the large coat hooks in the hallway. For example, the position of his coat would move and his hat would go missing for days on end. The umbrellas that were nestled in the stand by the front door would often topple over when they had never done so before. The family sheep dog Barney would often sit and bark at Polly. He said, *"He would just sit looking at the doll, barking. We didn't know what to make of it, but he seemed to be following something with his eyes. He would look from the doll across the room towards the doorway just as if he were watching someone walking. A friend of mine told me that dogs can see ghosts, so after that I wanted rid of her!"*

In February 2010, after having Polly for just over 12 months, the Evans family contacted us and asked us to visit them and take a look at the doll.

When we arrived Mrs Evans took us into the kitchen where Polly was sitting on a shelf. As we entered, we all felt a cold chill sweep through the room, just as if a window were open. Mrs Evans checked throughout the house and none were, so we immediately felt that we were possibly dealing with a paranormal connection. Kathleen, our psychic medium, approached the doll and as she reached up to fetch her down, the doll fell from the shelf of its own accord. This was a first for us as we had never before witnessed such immediate activity in the presence of a spirit.

We handled her very carefully as we all felt that we were being watched the whole time that we were in her presence. We took the doll into the dining room where we placed her on the large farmhouse table in front of the window. As we drew the curtains and began setting up our equipment, the light bulb blew. We asked if the Evans's could check their fuse box, but the switch to the dining room hadn't tripped and all other lights were working fine. The bulb was changed and the same thing happened again. We decided to use lamps and torches from this point onwards, and apart from one more lamp bulb blowing two hours into the session, we had no further problems with the lights, at least not that night!

Over the course of the next five days where we stayed with the Evans's, we established that there was indeed a spirit connected with the doll. A young girl aged ten by the name of Annabelle came forwards. Kathleen managed to call upon Annabelle successfully several times, and we all witnessed her appear in the form of an apparition.

Kathleen discovered that Annabelle had once lived in the very same farmhouse and that she had drowned in a nearby stream whilst out playing with her brother. She did not tell us why she was connected with this particular doll, but we felt that it may be because she simply liked it. The doll is not circa 19th century and so Annabelle must have noticed it years later when its original owner was playing with it.

The Evans's felt that her story was a bit too close to home for comfort and asked us to return to our home with the doll.

The Dybbuk Box

This box was discovered by the owners of a 19th-century

property in rural Worcestershire, whilst they were digging foundations in the properties rear garden.

A Dibbuk, or Dybbuk is from Jewish folklore. In essence, a dybbuk is a malicious or malevolent possessing spirit believed to be the dislocated soul of a dead person.

The information that follows includes testimonies from a couple we will name John and Irene to protect their identity. These statements were recorded with their permission during our initial visit to their home, and we have obtained permission to document the facts and the photographs they took at the time.

We were called to investigate this box after the couple who found it began experiencing horrific nightmares and disturbing visions. John who was in his late 50s had been digging up the old yard outside his Victorian property in order to lay foundations for a new patio area.

About three feet down his spade hit something solid and he uncovered the wooden box. After dusting it off, John took it indoors. He and his wife were intrigued by the box as it was bound with twine, almost as if somebody didn't want it to be opened. They weren't sure what to do with it so they decided to leave it whilst John continued with his work.

As Irene began to prepare the tea that night she remembered feeling very uneasy. The box was sitting on her dresser in the kitchen.

Irene: *"I felt like the box was watching me. I know that sounds stupid, how a box can watch you, but it just made me feel very uneasy and I had to put it somewhere out of the way."*

The box was found three feet underground.

Irene moved the box into the cellar and decided to leave it there until John figured out what he wanted to do with it. It was a few days later that John and Irene began experiencing problems with electrical equipment in their home.

John: *"We had just had a new kitchen fitted and had a new cooker, microwave and fridge. Within a few days of each other, they all stopped working. We couldn't believe it. We called the engineers in who said there was no explanation as all of the major parts were still functioning. They replaced them anyway, but I think we were all a bit confused about the whole thing."*

John decided one evening to go down into the cellar and have a better look at the box. He tried the switch to his cellar light but it wouldn't work, so he fetched a torch from the kitchen and down he went. In the gloom of the cellar, out of the corner of his eye he saw something run across the cellar.

John: *"It went from left to right, straight past me. It was too big for an animal, and seemed to be standing on two legs, like a man. I felt a breeze as it ran past me. It really shook me up".*

Irene: *"He [John] came running up from the cellar in a right state. He said someone was down there. I didn't know what to think. My first thought was that we had a squatter or a burglar or something. I called the police straight away."*

The police arrived and immediately checked the cellar. They found nothing. As standard procedure dictated, they took a statement from the couple before leaving.

John: *"They must have thought I was crazy, but I know what I saw."*

The following evening Irene bought the box up from the cellar, cut away the string that bound it together and opened it.

Irene: *"I immediately felt heaviness in the air. It was as if I had done something bad, something I shouldn't have done. I can't explain it but I felt guilty."*

The contents of the box

Irene and John took the box outside and examined the items inside it. They documented its contents by taking the photograph above.

Inside they found:

A small silver coloured candlestick
A brass coloured pot bound with string
A tooth
A small, glass drinking cup, which looked burnt on the base
A handmade wooden cross
A white shell
A few twigs and some kind of herbs
A broken wooden horseshoe

Authors note: *It is not clear what each item may have been used for, but a drinking vessel, candleholder and herbs are all items that are often found in ritualistic boxes or upon altars. The brass pot is probably the most fascinating of all of the items that were found inside the box as you can hear something soft move around inside when it is shaken. However, as it is bound neither John nor Irene wanted to open it.*

The next few weeks passed without incident until John began reporting that he was suffering from violent nightmares. He had never experienced anything remotely like this before. He recalls that around three weeks after they opened the box, he had a nightmare in which a man was watching him while he slept. He knew the man wanted something from him, and even though John knew it was a nightmare, he couldn't wake up.

John: *"I remember screaming to myself in the nightmare, wake up wake up it's just a dream, but I remained locked into this man's stare."*

He was eventually stirred by his wife Irene who had woken to the sounds of her husband crying out in his sleep. John didn't have this dream every night, but when he did, he reported that the man would visit him and either sit at the foot of the bed or stand over him, watching him intently.

John: *"Sometimes I felt like I couldn't breathe, as if there was some heavy force upon my chest. Other times I wouldn't see his face at all, just his eyes."*

John and Irene didn't make the connection with the box as they assumed that John was going through a period of stress.

Over the months that followed the couple experienced many disturbing things including visions, hallucinations, nightmares and headaches. Not only this, but John also began to notice physical changes. He found his hair began to fall out, his eyes seemed to have become much more bloodshot than usual and he became extremely sensitive to light. He also developed a slight tremble in his right hand.

Irene: *"He had the general appearance of someone 20 years his senior; we couldn't understand what was happening."*

John: *"I felt tired all the time and the disturbed sleep didn't help."*

They decided that the box must have had some kind of curse or bad luck associated with it and were determined to rid them of it. They tried to sell it at a car boot sale but no one wanted it. They threw it into the bin only to find it waiting for them at the front door. After conducting some online research they got in touch with us.

Upon Arrival
When we arrived at the property we felt a very heavy presence

within their home. There was an odour to the place a little like rotten fish. Irene said she had found it impossible to locate the source of the smell and that they had turned the house upside down and cleaned absolutely everywhere, but it had still come back stronger than ever.

John handed the box to our psychic Kathleen, whose hand twitched upon touching it almost as though she had received an electric shock. We knew we were dealing with something very different here, something that we had little to no experience of, but we agreed to take the box away with us. John and Irene explained that they had re-bound the box with its original string but the problems were still happening.

Research Around Jewish Dybbuk Boxes

Dybbuk boxes usually contain the soul of a demon that has been captured and contained within the box in order to protect us. After several sessions with this particular box we believe that the spirit is now safely contained once more. There have been no further occurrences.

We have been in touch with John and Irene and they have not experienced anything negative for the past 12 weeks to date. They have commented that the atmosphere within their home has lifted and they feel they can now "breathe again".

First LIVE Spirit Doll Experiment

20/10/2013

On 20th October 2013 several owners of dolls with attachments came together via Facebook to hold the very first Spirit Doll Communication Experiment. The aim of the experiment was to test the ability of our spirit dolls to share information through telepathy, amongst them. Our subject doll for the experiment was Mia.

Mia

This is the list of all other spirits that took part in the experiment as provided by their owners.

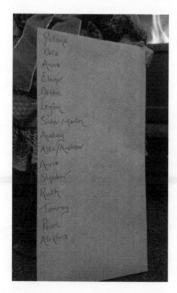

The spirits that gathered to take part in our live experiment.

Each person that wished to take part was required to upload a photograph of their chosen sprit doll and their name in advance of the experiment. This was to ensure that Mia was aware of who she was being asked to communicate with before the experiment began.

At 7.10pm we each of us joined a LIVE Facebook group chat accompanied by our chosen dolls.

Once ready, each person prepared their doll by explaining what was going to happen to them. Jayne then sat quietly with Mia and asked her to create a drawing through her. Upon completion of the drawing, Jayne asked Mia to 'show' this drawing to the spirits who inhabited the other dolls that were taking part in this experiment. At this point, Jayne's drawing was not shown to any one taking part in the experiment.

Jayne's drawing (as instructed by Mia).

Once completed, Jayne advised everybody involved to ask their spirit doll to show them what Mia had drawn in the hope that Mia's spirit had communicated the image with at least one of the other spirits taking part.

Once each person had drawn what they felt they were being shown by their spirit doll, they were asked to upload their drawings to the live chat.

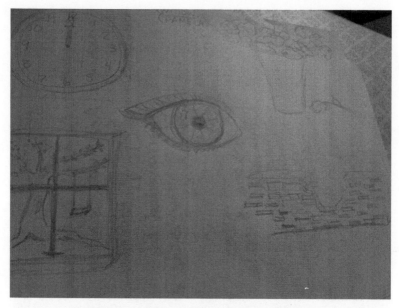

Pamela's drawing by Spirit Doll Willow.

Maria's drawing by Spirit Doll Shadow.

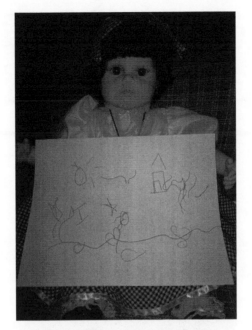

Sue's drawing by Spirit Doll Orla.

Zoes drawing by Spirit Doll Rebecca.

Troy's drawing by Spirit Doll Legion.

Stacey's drawing by Spirit Doll Tammy.

Marias drawing by Spirit Doll Shadow.

Conclusion

As you can see from Mia's original drawing, the main theme seems to involve trees, circles, stars and an eye. There were several drawings that follow this theme. Pamela's drawing, which was made via Willow, features both an eye and a tree. Victoria's drawing, which was made via Pearl, is also impressive as it shows an almost identical starburst effect.

Overall the participants of the experiment were really pleased with the results and believed that this experiment definitely goes some way to providing evidence that there may exist some form of communicative ability that is used by spirits.

Dolores
Origin: Evesham.
Came to us: 2009.
Attached Spirit: Dolores (Lori) – a woman in her late twenties.
Known activity: Doll changes position, induction of nightmare and migraines.

Dolores came to us for study in 2009. She originally kept watch over a tiny curiosity shop that was based in Evesham. Her owner Kathy had kept her sitting on a shelf to help *oversee* the day-to-day dealings of the shop. Kathy had never intended to sell her although many people had asked if she was for sale, she just felt that the doll belonged in the shop.

Kathy had taken out a lease on the shop 18 months prior to our visit and explained to us that whilst clearing space in the back storage room she had found a few dolls and toys boxed up. The shop had previously been a toyshop for over forty years.

She explained that she had split everything that she found between the three local charity shops, but something about this particular doll caught her attention and she couldn't bear to part with her.

Kathy found a spot for Dolores (at that time known as Sally) next to the shop's entrance. She even placed a notice card on her lap, which read, "Welcome to our shop, pat my head for luck." Kathy thought it to be a cute gimmick and of course had no idea what may ensue as a result.

Over the course of three or four weeks following the shops opening, Kathy began experiencing chronic migraines – though perhaps naturally she put this down to the stress of opening a new business. It was only when disturbing nightmares began to follow that Kathy started to worry. She explained to us that initially she had a psychic medium visit to bless the shop as she felt that maybe there was some residual energy left over from the previous tenants. The building itself was built in the 15th century and must have seen its fair share of high emotion. She told us that after this first blessing things settled for a few days. Then one morning when she opened up, Kathy noticed that 'Sally' was facing in the opposite direction. She assumed that she had brushed past her on the way out of the shop the night before and spun her without noticing. However, she continued to find the doll facing the opposite way morning after morning. Kathy started to get nervous being in the shop on her own, especially as she had now started to feel that someone was often standing next to her when she was positioned behind the counter. On one occasion she reported to us that the till had opened and two one pound coins had 'jumped' out of the drawer and landed at her feet.

This was the last straw for her and she called in a local paranormal team to check out the building. They spent three afternoons with her and each time their evidence proved inconclusive.

Unsure where to turn next Kathy tried to ignore things until five weeks later something happened that led her to contact us. One of her customers made a comment in passing that seemed to ring true to her. An elderly woman who had never been in the shop before remarked, *"You know she doesn't like being there don't you?"* Kathy dismissed the statement and the old lady said no more, but her words played on her mind and she moved the doll next to the till. Alas this made things significantly worse. Kathy talked of more coins being found on the floor around the till and of the receipt roll going crazy and churning out receipt after receipt! Kathy also reported that pens flew out of her pen pot on one occasion and that this really scared her as she was standing close by at the time.

She asked a local vicar to visit the shop and perform a short blessing. She hung a cross behind the counter and took to wearing her own silver crucifix – none of which seemed to make a difference.

(In cases where there is no demonic or dark presence, we have found that taking this kind of action rarely has any effect as we believe light energies, that is, once human souls, are not repelled by religion and its symbolism. Of course there are exceptions to this rule.)

We set up our equipment in the shop one Friday evening and waited in the hope we might capture something. Just before 1.30am we heard a sound coming from over by the counter. We moved slowly towards the till but nothing was being picked up by any of our equipment. As I approached the counter I placed the EMF meter down and asked if someone was with us. After a few quick flashes (indicating a strong fluctuation in the electromagnetic field around us), there was nothing. Then as we were all about to retake our seats the till began to 'beep' as if someone were pressing the keys. Kathy was frozen with fear. At this point Hazel (our psychic medium) began to recite a short prayer in the hope that the activity would cease. The till continued to 'beep'. Hazel wrote 'STOP' on a piece of paper and placed it next to the till and silence followed. I had never before witnessed the effect of written requests on spirit activity and Hazel later explained to me that occasionally spoken words often get lost in the atmosphere, especially if there is high emotion involved. This is often why asking a spirit to show themselves or to stop will have no effect. The session ended just before 2am and Kathy decided that she would rather not take part in any further investigations.

The following night we repeated the process and this time a young woman came forward to Hazel following a request for communication via pendulum. Hazel kept her stare firmly fixed on the counter behind me as she spoke aloud.

After just over 20 minutes of communication we had noted that the presence was that of a woman in her late 20s named Dolores. She referred to herself initially as Lori. Hazel asked for clarification, which is when her true name was presented.

Following that final session in the shop it was agreed that we would bring Dolores back with us for further work. Kathy has since reported that the atmosphere in her shop has lifted and she no longer experiences anything out of the ordinary.

Dolores remains an ongoing challenge, as she is known to retreat from questioning for prolonged periods, meaning that building a full picture of her life is difficult. For now, she remains with us.

Handheld Divination Mirror

History:
This item had been passed through five generations of gypsy

travellers and was said to have been used to connect with the dead and to help predict the future. The exact age of the mirror is unknown but it bears the characteristics of certain medieval styles.

Front face of the mirror.

Rear face of the mirror.

This mirror came into our possession in 2006 after visiting a young traveller girl in her community, which was situated within Liverpool. She had inherited the mirror from her grandmother, who in turn had been given it by her mother. She was told that the wise women within the community in previous generations had used the mirror to see through to the spirit world, communicate with the dead and to predict the future.

The young girl (who for the purposes of this book I shall call Dawn) had no interest in the afterlife, having being raised within the modern ways of travelling life. She actually told us that she feared what the mirror represented and that she no longer wanted it in her home. The final straw regarding Dawn's relationship with the mirror came when she began seeing a woman within the mirror at first and then later in her dreams. The woman seemed old and haggard and Dawn felt that the energy associated with her was largely negative. She would try to wake herself from the nightmares that featured the old crone, but was often unable to do so.

She began to experience other phenomena around her home. Taps would run in the middle of the night, seemingly of their own accord. She would see shadows, and ornaments would rattle and vibrate for no apparent reason. She felt sure that somebody or something was trying to get her attention.

Dawn began to experience feelings of guilt in relation to the mirror. She felt that she was not using the mirror for its intended purpose, and that by leaving it sitting in a drawer she was neglecting the mirror and its unique history. She believed that all of the activity that she was experiencing was related to this feeling, and that this was the message that the spirit within the mirror was trying to convey to her. She confronted her mother about the mirror and asked if she had ever tried using it to look into the future. Although her mother had been raised in the old traditions of the travellers, she was inherently afraid of the paranormal and would not have the mirror in her home.

The gypsy community are a very proud and superstitious people. Once word spread that a spirit connected with the mirror was trying to make contact, everybody that Dawn knew told her to get rid of it. She was told many tales about the mirror and its past including one where the Devil used the mirror to trick its owner into believing that she could see the future.

We were contacted in late November and asked if we would be willing to visit Dawn. When we first met her she was holding the mirror in her hand. Her first words to us were, "Do you know what this is?" She then went on to tell us the history associated with the piece, explained about the nightmares that she was suffering from, and why she could no longer keep the mirror in her home.

We agreed to take it for study. She requested that we did not contact her with details of our findings.

We initially held one-to-one sessions with the mirror where we asked any spirits associated with the item to come forward and using our pendulum for to aid in communication. The results gathered her were inconclusive.

It was only when we gathered our team together for a group session that things really started to happen. In our first session Kathleen (our psychic medium) placed her hands over the mirror and asked that any spirits that wished to come through do so by channelling through both the mirror and her. After about a minute a very fine mist seemed to escape the surface of the mirror and rise towards her hands. Suddenly she moved her hands away and requested that we close the session immediately. Later she described how she had felt a very strong energy come forward. The energy was female and had attempted to take control of the session through Kathleen.

Our research suggested that mirrors were often used in séances as a tool for communication with the deceased.

We experienced high EMF readings during group sessions

and lower results during our one-to-one sittings. We concluded that the item needed a large amount of energy surrounding it in order for it to become active.

It was discovered that the mirror was used by many mediums, psychics and clairvoyants during its time, which meant that there could potentially be several spirits at any one time attempting communication by way of it.

We concluded that the mirror held the energy to become a very strong portal between this world and the next.

Connie

Origin: London, UK.

Joined us: January 2010.

Known Spirit: A young British woman called Connie, who died in 1879, allegedly at the hands of her father who was a colonel with the British Army.

Activity displayed: Cold rushes of air, occasional singing (though this is rare). Likes to move small objects.

Vessel: Doll dressed in beautiful Victorian-Indian style clothing comprising of a cream satin trouser suit with lace trim. She has red hair and green eyes.

This doll was originally called Maggie by her owner but she renamed her Connie after connecting with her spirit.

She came to us in 2009 after her owner Marguerite had passed away. Fiona, who was the daughter of Marguerite was busy arranging the house clearance when she reported that things started to move around (though it was only small objects such as glasses, ornaments and keys etc). Over the next few days, whenever Fiona was in her mother's home, she recorded that her car keys went missing before reappearing three times, her toothbrush moved from the sink to the bedroom twice, and her hairpins were always scattered on the floor in the morning. Being a religious woman she was not frightened by these things and assumed that it was her mother letting her know that she was still present.

According to what Fiona told us when we first met her in December of 2009, her mother came to her in a dream and kept talking about 'the doll' and mentioning the name 'Connie'.

"She was telling me to look after Connie," Fiona recalls. "I had no idea who she meant, and when she kept mentioning *the doll* I assumed she meant Maggie." Marguerite had owned Maggie for 10 years and had been very fond of her, although she had never mentioned that her actual name was indeed Connie.

Fiona sold most of the contents of the house very quickly, but she kept a hold of a jewellery box, a few of her mother's clothes, and Maggie the doll. "No one wanted it," Fiona told us. "I just assumed it had gone out of fashion and no one was really collecting them anymore." Fiona went on to explain that she had heard someone comment upon passing the stall where the doll had sat on sale that it *gave them the creeps*.

With the doll now unsold it went to live with Fiona at her flat in London and there it remained. For two months nothing happened. There were no unusual occurrences and Fiona thought no more about the strange goings on that she had experienced at her mother's house. Then one night in late December 2009, Fiona awoke at 3am. She was freezing cold.

"I know it was winter, but I had my heating up and a winter duvet on my bed. I shouldn't have been cold at all, but I was freezing. My fingers and toes were numb and I couldn't get warm."

Fiona went to check on the boiler, and everything was fine. As she moved through the flat back to the bedroom, she felt someone watching her. When she turned, Connie was on the floor, sitting against the wall, staring directly at her.

"It freaked me out. I'm not a doll person anyway, something about the eyes, and I certainly did not like the way that doll was looking at me."

The next day Fiona felt incredibly sad but she couldn't put her finger on as to why. She felt that there was heaviness within the air of the flat.

Three nights later she dreamt of her mother and things began to make sense. Her mother explained to Fiona, that Connie was a lady who had never passed over to the other side after death and that she had spent years believing that she was still alive. She had no desire to be dead at all and so remained on this side of life.

"When I dreamt of my mother, she told me that this Connie lady was using the doll as a vessel. A way to remain here safely. I couldn't believe it at first but then it was like the last piece of a jigsaw slotted into place, and I knew instantly, that it was true."

Fiona was initially uncomfortable with the thought of Connie sharing her home and decided to conduct some research into spirit attachment. "I didn't want to simply throw her away as I know she meant so much to my mother, but I also knew I couldn't keep her."

We visited Fiona on January 19th, 2010 and took Connie away for two nights in order to study her. After conducting numerous tests using infrared and night vision surveillance, monitoring changes in room temperature and extended EVP sessions we were able to conclude that Connie was displaying signs of paranormal activity. We advised Fiona of our findings and it was agreed that we would purchase Connie.

In the time that we owned her we have heard the sound of a lady singing in the room where Connie is kept, and as Fiona reported, we have had small items go missing throughout the house. After many sittings with this spirit, we concluded that Connie has come to terms with her passing, and is much happier since she told her story to us. She is shy and gentle, and loves to be amongst us in our world.

Historical Detail Provided by Connie

In the various séances that we conducted with Connie, she spoke with us largely via the use of a pendulum and passed on details about her life in India under the rule of her father. She was unhappy at the treatment that the local people received and embarrassed her father by cooking her own food alongside the servants. She was an independent lady and believes in equality for all. When these issues are discussed within her company the energy in the room becomes noticeably heavier.

Elenor

Origin: Wiltshire, UK.

Joined us: April 2006.

Known Spirit: A 24-year-old aristocratic woman who died broken hearted after her fiancé fell in love with another woman.

Activity displayed: The sound of crying, doll changing position, and owners dreaming of Elenor. Electrical items around her are activated by unseen hands and light bulbs often flicker in her presence. Most people coming into contact with the doll say they feel a sense of anguish in her presence.

Elenor almost did not make it into our collection. When her original owner contacted us she explained that she had been experiencing electrical problems in her home (such as flickering lights in her hallway and bedroom), which only occurred when Elenor was positioned nearby.

After studying the doll for two months our findings proved inconclusive. The owner was disappointed upon hearing this and

**It has been said that the pain Elenor holds is evident
in her face.**

maintained that the doll was responsible for the series of strange electrical occurrences in her home.

Two days after returning the doll, the owner had a dream in which a woman (later confirmed as Elenor) came to her and apologised for her upsetting behaviour. Elenor went on to tell her that she felt at home within the doll and if she was uncomfortable with her residing inside it, then she was sorry for making her feel this way.

After a call from the owner explaining this latest development we agreed to go back and visit the doll again. Using the information that the owner had provided us with we spoke aloud and asked for *Elenor* to come forward. We told her that we were not there to harm her and that we simply wanted to see proof that she was actually with us. Within 30 seconds of speaking the doll had fallen from the table and the light bulbs above had flickered and burst. The air went cold and we knew at that moment that Elenor was with us.

Information Gathered through Our Studies

Elenor was very reluctant to show herself as a full apparition as she felt *unworthy* of our attention. However, she would relay information to us, and over time, as she began to trust us, she began appearing. (The appearances only lasted for a very short periods. In total she appeared to us three times.)

Elenor remained with us for a long time. She is very special and required much patience and care. Elenor has never recovered from losing her beloved. Over the years we have had several psychic mediums contact Elenor and try to send her into the light, but she never seems to be able to quite manage to cross over. Sometimes it is believed to be more difficult when spirits are broken-hearted as they have a desire to remain on this side of life until they finally feel at peace. Elenor was incredibly sad when she came to us, and she affected me personally (I used to cry quite a lot as I found that I picked up on her feelings – Jayne).

She is sometimes friendly and interactive, other times quiet. However, her feelings of sadness and loss are ever present.

Bobby:
Origin: Unknown, arrived anonymously.
Joined us: August 2014.
Known Spirit: A boy, aged 9.
Activity displayed: Objects fall to the floor, there are strange

shuffling sounds when in isolation, temperature fluctuations, and strange visuals on night vision (see photos).

Unlike most items we research, this doll comes with no history or information prior to its arrival.

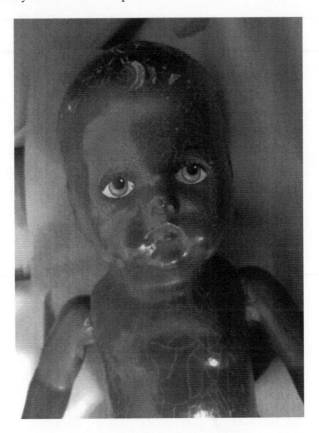

Bobby

This doll came to us anonymously in a plain brown package. There was no note or return address attached.

Initial 24 Hours

As is our standard procedure, the doll was placed in the isolation cabinet for 24 hours. A noted temperature drop of three degrees was noted within 30 minutes of this isolation phase commencing.

During the first night, Jayne and her husband were awoken at 3am by a loud bang that had come from downstairs. Upon investigation nothing was found. As they returned to the bedroom there was another bang, this time originating from the cellar. They collected the night vision equipment and descended the cellar steps. As they did so a swift chill passed them by. There were no known draughts anywhere to explain this. As they moved closer towards the study area (and the isolation cabinet) they felt a heaviness in the air. Jayne reported hearing someone behind her and as she turned back towards the steps, she sensed someone watching her. She instinctively used the night vision camera and captured what she believed to be a presence that seemed to alter the appearance of the image.

Initial image taken under 'normal' conditions.

Image captured during heavy atmosphere.

Jayne and her husband turned and moved closer to the study area though nothing more was experienced.

Aftermath

The doll was moved out of the cabinet and was placed onto a step in the cellar for further observation. Upon moving the doll, there appeared to be a damp patch around him. This remained for several days and could not be explained.

There followed several days of no activity. The case was discussed with Hazel (our psychic medium) and Jayne explained that she was concerned that a possible malevolent energy was in association with the doll based upon the oppressive atmosphere experienced during the first 24 hours. She visited the doll and attempted to communicate. She was unable to establish contact to a level that she could comfortably engage the spirit, but she explained that there was a light energy in association and to expect an according sign or gift.

The next week a small white feather was found at the door to the cellar. Hazel confirmed that this was the sign that the energy attached to the doll was one of light and not darkness.

A sign from the light?

Findings

Through repeated interactions using the pendulum, EMF meters, group sessions and one-to-one sessions we have documented that the spirit in attachment is male, aged nine (or there about), who died as the result of a vicious attack. Hazel has described a vulnerability that she sensed quite strongly from him. She has attempted on several occasions to establish exactly what happened to him and who was responsible, but unfortunately he was not forthcoming with this information. When questioned further, activity lessened and at times communication ended (as one might expect when interrogating a child).

Silver & Turquoise Aztec Design Signet Ring
Came to us: 2009.
Origin: Norfolk.
Known Spirits: A previous owner Thomas who died in a motorbike accident aged 16.

The ring was found within a large jewellery box that was purchased from a house clearance specialist who had recently cleared a house in Norfolk. It was said that the entire contents of the house were being sold and that the money raised was to be donated to a children's charity, as per the request of Louisa, the last remaining family member.

Louisa suffered from dementia and was to move into a

residential care home just before her 86th birthday. This was how her belongings came to be put up for sale. We studied all of the pieces that we came across, but none gave us any reactions until we tested the ring pictured above.

Initial tests showed that the ring produced higher than normal EMF readings and we wondered whether the stone itself was causing this reaction by somehow manipulating the magnetic fields around it. It wasn't until around eight weeks that other activity began to manifest.

Hazel (our medium) called in one morning to report that she had been visited in her dreams during the night by a young man who had suffered the most terrible injures to his face and neck. She described the ring that he was wearing – silver with a bright blue stone. Up until this point Hazel had not seen the ring that we had purchased from the house sale. The ring was presented to her and she burst into tears. That was the same ring that she had seen the young man wearing in her dream.

Hazel took it home and kept it for a couple of weeks. In that time she reported that she had some wonderful interactions with the spirit of Thomas. Although he did not ever appear to her, Hazel felt that he was audibly present for three consecutive nights. At 11:30 each evening she would feel his presence. She later discovered that this was the precise time of his motorcycle accident.

Once the ring was returned there was a sudden wave of activity, which often included the strong smell of engine oil. On other occasions a very distinctive aftershave could be smelt around the house and this was often accompanied by sudden and unexplained drops in temperature. Thomas was apparently unaware that he had passed over until Hazel worked with him. The offer of assisted passage was made to which he declined.

17th Century Gentleman's Signet Ring
Origin: South London. Hidden behind a cavity wall.

Came to us: 2007.

Known Attachments: An unknown gentleman.

The ring above was discovered hidden within a Victorian property in South London by a property developer in 2007. It was taken to a local jeweller to be identified; however, identification of the signet stamp or exact age of the ring could not be determined. It is believed to be 17th century in origin.

The ring came into Jayne's possession via a dealership auction. She sensed that the ring was special and was happy to add it to her collection.

It was soon discovered that the ring had belonged to an important gentleman. A tall figure wearing a top hat was witnessed on several occasions whilst working with this ring. A strong, herb-like odour was often detected, which Jayne and her team determined to be that of snuff.

This ring would have probably been worn on the little or ring finger and contains a strong energy (one of the strongest that Jayne has witnessed from a piece of jewellery!). Each of the team has spent time with this ring and all have dreamt of the same man. He is always seen standing with his cane in the streets of London. Further investigation into why the ring should come to be in a Victorian property and what happened to its original owner has proven futile. The ring and its owner remain a mystery.

Sarah
Origin: Preston, UK.
Joined us: June 2013.
Activity displayed: Gentle movement noted (this clown doll sits on a swing), strong smell of cinnamon that comes and goes, high EMF readings, varying pendulum activity, communicative with professional medium through tarot cards and spirit board.

This clown doll came to us in June 2013 following a sudden and unexplained period of activity reported by its owner. (For the purposes of privacy we shall refer to the previous owner as Ted.) Ted had owned the clown doll for several years and had a fascination with clowns. He couldn't recall from where he had purchased it, but it was definitely second-hand.

Ted had hung the clown in his second bedroom, which was used as a guest room. Ted rarely had guests, as he explained to us during our initial visit, but when friends did stay with him, they always asked that he take the clown doll down or cover the face.

When we visited Ted it had been a warm day. We entered the bedroom where the clown was kept and were immediately struck by the difference in temperature. We checked on the digital thermometer and there had been a drop of three degrees. We usually look for logical explanations for changes in temperature, but on seeing the rest of the house, we realized the bedroom was central and had only one outside wall.

We asked Ted if he had a window open or if the window had been open at all during the day, but when he showed us the old metal frames were 'welded' closed with layers and layers of old paint, we knew he was being truthful when he said that he hadn't. The clown was not the only doll in the room. There were also two porcelain dolls on the windowsill, but they seemed of no significance in terms of atmospheric effect.

Hazel instinctively walked towards the clown doll and placed a hand on him (at that time any spirit present had been assumed as male). When she looked back towards us we knew she felt a presence.

As with all new cases, we asked Ted if he would like us to work with him in his home initially. Some owners prefer this. Ted, however, had no desire to communicate or to know more about it. We therefore agreed to take the clown, and Hazel performed a thorough house cleansing to help put Ted at ease. She later told us during the car journey home that Ted had two other spirits in his home but they were residual (meaning their energy was merely left over from their life previously in that home) and of no concern.

Once home we worked with the clown in the usual way for several months but were unable to gain much detail. For some reason we had felt the entity to be male. Possibly because we have found this to generally is the case when dealing with clown dolls with spirit attachment. However, it has since came to light that the soul attached to the clown is named Sarah.

In establishing and verifying details in this case, we called upon the help of psychic medium Chris Croker-Corber.

Chris has performed several divination sessions on our behalf and has confirmed the following:

Chris first connected via spirit board. It was established that the spirit was female, and friendly (a light energy).

Born in April 1947. Died in June 1964.

She indicated to Chris that she died of an illness, which was later established as depression. It also emerged that her cause of death was suicide. When Chris questioned Sarah about the 'cause' of her depression, she simply said, "Life."

Chris then entered a meditative state and asked why Sarah chose to ground herself in this particular vessel, the answer came very intuitively. She said in life she wished to please people and to make them happy.

For his next session, Chris used a pendulum and pendulum board to gain the following confirmations:

Are you male? No
Are you female? Yes
Is your name Sarah? Yes
Were you born in 1947? Yes
Were you born in March? No
Were you born in April? Yes

This confirmed to us that we had made contact with the right spirit.

Chris later used his Oracle and Tarot cards to read for Sarah. Here are his discoveries, in his words.

I shuffled the Oracle cards and asked Sarah to tell me when to stop. The Oracle card chosen told me that Sarah likes to make new friends and she is very protective over the people she loves. Then I got out my Rider-Waite tarot deck to see if we could do the same, but this time I decided to do a 3-card spread.

1st card (Personal). The card drawn indicated that Sarah found it difficult to conform to societies ideal of what was normal.

2nd card (Social). This card indicated that in life Sarah was a people pleaser and liked to ensure the happiness of others (confirming what she had previously said about her choice of vessel.)

3rd card (Spiritual) indicated that Sarah was upset with how woman were treated in her family and she was unable to feel comfortable in her own skin i.e. femininity and sexuality due to the strong beliefs of her family.

Once Chris had provided us with this information, I held a pendulum session with Sarah, and asked her to confirm her name. We got a definite swing towards the letter 'S'. I was thrilled. Chris had mentioned to ask Sarah about 'Anna' as this name had also come up. I asked if she was Anna, to which she replied, "Yes." This was confusing at first but Chris later cleared this up when he held a spirit board session and Sarah indicated that Anna is her friend; a girl aged 18, also in spirit.

The Lady in the Brooch
Joined us: 2003.
Origin: Unknown.

This brooch holds the energy of one of the most interesting spirits we have encountered to date. Lady Catherine lived in the 1800s and mysteriously vanished aged 22. This information was gathered and confirmed using a wide variety of divination methods, that all began and ended with a group séance session.

Catherine had been a very religious woman; she was a devout Catholic and a woman who knew her own mind. She had strong views on a variety of issues, and she had indicated to us via our medium that she was a strong believer in freedom of speech and women's rights.

Communication with Catherine had largely been through the forms of dream visitation and though group séances. A pendulum was the main tool used during these particular sessions. Through the use of the pendulum and Hazel's dream records, we had established that Catherine vanished from her home (site unknown) on 22nd March 1835. She still held a degree of sadness as she knew that her family looked for her for many years, but their search proved fruitless. Communication sessions tended to break suddenly when we attempted to explore exactly what happened to Catherine.

The brooch came into our possession in 2003 and was one of the first items that we worked with that was not a doll. It came with no prior background at as it was purchased purely by chance at a flea market in Stow-on-the-Wold, The Cotswolds. When we bought it back home we were astounded by the level of activity we experienced during the first 24 hours as it is not often that we experience energy strong enough to physically move an object.

It was placed where it would be not be disturbed, surrounded by trigger objects and safely within the confines of a salt circle. Some hours later one of the small trigger objects had been moved, but stranger still, the salt circle had been broken and the brooch was face down.

On day six of our ownership of the brooch, my husband began experiencing vivid dreams. In these dreams a woman would come to him and speak of a brooch. She told him she was not content with its treatment. He felt strongly that she didn't want it to be studied or kept in the manner we were keeping it. In the final dream that he experienced, the woman appeared to him wearing the brooch. She made it clear to him that it must be worn.

We started to keep the brooch with us either by wearing it or by keeping it in a pocket, wallet or bag. Whenever I carried it I would begin to feel light-headed, and had visual disturbances that I couldn't explain. I cannot say in all honesty that it was a pleasant experience as I found it disturbing at times. My husband and I began to experience scents, sounds and images of a past life that we could not easily explain. Neither of us is psychic, but it seemed to us that an ability of Catherine's was perhaps being shared with us in some way via our connection with her brooch.

We were advised by a spiritualist group to keep the brooch in a safe place and to limit its wear. It was occasionally used as a communication aid or divination tool.

June

Origin: Lyon, France.

Joined us: April, 2004.

Known Spirit: June (aged 25). *She has appeared on several occasions in spirit form. She resembles this doll in appearance with fair features and shorter hair.*

Activity displayed: The sound of sobbing is a regular occurrence as is dream visitation and electrical interference. Most people coming into contact with the doll say they feel a sense of sadness followed by joy.

June has been with us since 2004. She is very special and requires patience, and we almost did not take June into our collection.

When her original owner contacted us she had been experiencing a lot of electrical problems in her home including flickering lights in her hallway and bedroom that only occurred in the presence of the doll. We visited the property but could gain no satisfactory evidence of anything paranormal. We agreed to study June, and over a period of two weeks conducted the usual tests on her. Again our findings were inconclusive.

Her owner was disappointed with our results and felt very strongly that the doll was responsible for the strange occurrences in her home. Two days after we left the doll, her owner had a dream in which a woman named June came to her and apologised for her upsetting behaviour. June told her that she felt 'at home' with the doll and could not leave.

The following morning we received a call and agreed to go back to visit. Using the information that the owner had provided we asked June to come forward. We told her we were not there to harm her and simply wanted proof that she was really with us. Within 30 seconds the doll had fallen from the table and the lights in the adjoining room had briefly flickered before two of the four bulbs burst. The air went noticeably colder, which was confirmed by temperature readings, and we knew at that moment, that June was with us.

We are not 100 per cent sure how June came to be in the spirit world although we do know that she wants desperately to care for children. She is a bit of a lost soul. Over the years we have had several psychic mediums contact June and try to send her into the light but she never manages to cross over. She simply does not want to go.

Three years ago a psychic medium made contact with June and asked her several questions. Whilst in a meditative state the psychic medium saw blue skies and we have found that positioning June close by a window helps control spirit activity within the owners home.

Maddie
Origin: Bridgnorth.
Came to us: 2004.

We have many had experiences as a result of our ongoing work; some inevitably leave a lasting impression as they bring with them a lesson learnt. This doll taught us one of those lessons. (*I should point out that we have had her in a protective casing for over 10 years and only take her out for controlled sessions. The reason for this is that Maddie is HIGHLY active. Of course a standard glass cabinet cannot hold back the type of force we have witnessed from Maddie, however, once blessed, purified and anointed with holy water (once a month) we found her calmer, especially since our children arrived.*)

Maddie remains isolated in the basement.

Maddie likes fires, which is odd as she died in a house fire in

1901. We have been assured that she WILL NOT cause fires as this is not one of her noted activities. However, the smell of burning is not uncommon when she is present.

When conducting group sessions with Maddie it was suggested that we should occasionally bring her upstairs and hold séances next to the open fire. When we tried this we received a notable increase in responses to our questions. We have a few theories around why this may be the case, but we are yet to settle upon a satisfactory one. It is clear though, that there is something about this spirit that is encouraged by the presence of fire.

We found Maddie in an antique shop in Bridgnorth, Shropshire in 2004. She was housed at the bottom of a tall cabinet with an assortment of other objects and had been there for some time. I had seen her on several occasions over a period of about four months and it seemed that no one wanted her. However, that changed one Sunday morning. I was browsing and my mother saw the doll. She told me I should take her home as she didn't like being in the shop because she didn't like the owner! It was said light-heartedly at the time, but somehow I couldn't leave the shop without her. We haggled and I got her for a reduced price (probably as the owner was fed up of having her there!). As I returned home in the car I kept looking back at her as I couldn't shake the feeling that I was being watched.

When I got home, for some reason or another I didn't go through the usual process of isolation. I knew or at least I believed that she wouldn't approve of this treatment. It felt as close to having a 'real' person in my home as I've ever experienced.

I made sure to change her location a few times. I tend to do with this with all of our new dolls in order to get a sense of where they are happiest. In every location I sensed dissatisfaction.

We settled upon our bedroom for a while. However, she

started getting too disruptive. Nothing would remain on our bedroom walls, no pictures, paintings, not even a very lightweight canvas that hung above her. All would constantly fall down or be removed. Some nights my perfume bottles would rattle and would only stop if I told her I was unhappy with the way that she was behaving. I took comfort from the fact that she did seem to have a level of respect for our home and us, and concluded that she was restless or maybe even a little frightened.

Our first group session with Maddie (who at this point was still nameless) was held on 3rd November 2003, a date which I shall never forget. We gathered a group of five people for the initial sitting. Myself, my husband, psychic medium Hazel, and two other friends who had shown an interest in the paranormal, all sat around the Ouija board. *(Ouija boards are not a divination method we advocate, and no longer use ourselves, as although they seem to provide responses and results, we have since learnt that these cannot always be relied upon. Their effectiveness relies on the opening of a portal, a doorway, which once open, will remain open unless closed down by someone experienced. In our experience an open portal can act as an invitation to entities that may be unwelcome.)* It was 11.30pm when we began. The doll itself was perched on a shelf above us.

Hazel started by performing a protection blessing and then asked a series of questions, looking for movement to indicate a response. At first nothing of note was recorded. Then suddenly and without warning, the doll fell from its place above us and landed with a thud in the centre of the Ouija board. We looked at each with shared excitement as to what may follow. At this point the temperature was noted at a steady 19 degrees. The doll was placed back onto the shelf and left in a secure position.

The session continued for a further 20 minutes. It was at this point that Hazel commented that there was a smell of burning around us. Its exact location was a mystery, but it was unquestionably there. Wanting to avoid another break in concentration, Hazel proceeded to ask more questions. The smell intensified until we all agreed that it felt as though we were inhaling smoke. Not knowing whether or not the experience had been conjured by the spirit present with us, Hazel asked that all physical disturbances now cease. Upon her request a glow began to form in the centre of the board. It was about the size of a 50 pence coin, orange in colour and slowly increased in brightness. Everybody jumped back from the table assuming that the board was somehow alight. Hazel calmly requested that the spirit stop and the glow disappeared. The air lifted and the room fell measurably colder. Readings were now showing a temperature of 15 degrees. Upon checking the board we found no signs of burn marks. It was not even warm to touch.

In total the session lasted 55 minutes.

We gathered from the session that not only was there an obvious presence within the doll, but that it held a significant strength in terms of energy. We gained the letter 'M' from our requests for a name, and subsequent sessions provided us with confirmation that her name is Maddie. Pendulum divination provided us with the year 1933 and the knowledge that a fire was to blame for her passing at the age of 39.

Following a period of six months with living Hazel, Maddie was returned to us. She has been in our home and for the past 10 years and has safely resided behind glass in our basement. We still occasionally get the faint smell of burning when we are down there with her, although she is significantly 'calmer' than when she first came to us. Faint light anomalies have also been seen on several occasions above the doll. These are often said to indicate spirit presence.

Cases Where No Attachment is Recorded

It goes without saying that a huge proportion of the items that come into our possession are found to hold no measurable paranormal activity. This is an inevitable part of the work and further demonstrates how our minds can often convince us that something supernatural is occurring in our homes. The people we meet are all convinced that they have something paranormal occurring in their homes or workplace, so it's always interesting once we know there are no paranormal connections to an item, to look at possible 'natural' explanations.

Molly's Silver Ring

We were called to visit a lady named Molly in June 2010 after she had been experiencing vivid nightmares, waking hallucinations and dizziness. She had inherited a shell ring when her sister passed away six months prior to our visit and she had always felt that there was something unusual about it. She kept it in a small trinket box, and never wore it. Her sister had worn it regularly and Molly had always had her suspicions that her sister had dabbled in the occult.

Upon arriving at Molly's home we felt no obvious signs of spirit presence. Molly spoke at length about her experiences since having the ring in her home. She described her visions and night- mares and how they were affecting her on a daily basis. Her friends had told her to throw the ring  away, but she told us she had read somewhere that doing such a thing could bring about more unpleasant experiences.

Initial tests in her home were inconclusive. There were a few EMF fluctuations but alone these could be explained away. She seemed so affected by the presence of the ring that we agreed to take it away and let her know our findings.

Initially we placed trigger objects around the ring and a circle of salt. After 48 hours, there did appear to be a slight movement from one of the objects, but it was so slight that it could have easily been caused by vibrations in the home (doors slamming, people walking on floorboards above etc). All of these natural occurrences can cause very small vibrations meaning that the movement of trigger objects alone – unless showing significant movements – cannot be classed as a 'positive' result. The salt circle remained intact.

Next as part of our standard procedures, we invited Hazel to come and try psychometry with the ring. She held it for a while and although nothing immediately came to her, she wanted to work with it again later that evening. A few attempts at psychometry were made and Hazel told us that she had experienced a sense of fear on a few occasions. We determined this to simply be the feelings and emotions Molly had transferred to the item since owning it and not a sign of anything paranormal. Hazel is often able to detect emotions in association with objects.

A few more tests involving EVP attempts, K2 and pendulum sessions all resulted in little to no response.

We concluded that this ring whilst having a very strong psychological effect on Molly was not an item that contained any paranormal energy.

Advice for Those
Who are Considering Purchasing
an Item with a Spirit Attachment

Before making the decision to own an item that displays paranormal activity it is wise to do your research and be prepared.

The idea of owning such an item can be very appealing to some and incredibly frightening to others. Think about other people around you, especially those within your home. Are they equally as comfortable with the paranormal as you? How will they feel about a haunted or paranormally active item being in their home?

These are questions that you should ask and we have a responsibility to advise you to make these considerations.

Concerns for Those with Children and Pets

There is plenty of evidence to suggest that children and animals can be especially sensitive to spirits.

We would advise extra consideration if you have a child at home. Spirits often show particular interest in children as they are naturally more receptive. It may not bother you that your child may be able to see a spirit, and in our experience allowing children to be more spiritually aware is not necessarily a bad thing, but some may find this unsettling. Likewise, your pet may sense when a spirit is close. Consider if this would make you uncomfortable,

Seeking Help

We make every effort to ensure that we know the identity and characteristics of each spirit, but do bear in mind that spirits can be tricksters and it has been known (although we must emphasise that this is very rare) for a seemingly kind and gentle spirit to become angry. Should this occur we would advise you to contact your local spiritualist church for advice and ask that they come to your home to perform a blessing. We must stress that these instances are incredibly rare, and in over 16 years of dealing with the paranormal, we have only been made aware of three occasions in which outside help was needed.

Objects of this nature should be treated with respect. Trying to antagonize or mock the spirits in any way can lead to upset and confusion.

New Owners

New owners are advised to recite the following blessing when they receive their doll. This has been shown to aid a smooth transition from one place to another, and to reassure them that you mean them no harm.

> *Welcome* (spirits name) *into our home and thank you for allowing us the opportunity to protect you.*
> *May you feel peace, love and light always.*
> *We recognise your importance and respect you,*
> *Please roam freely,*
> (Here is a section in which you can mention any ground rules)
> *And above all be at home*
> *Many Blessings Always*
> —Written by Hazel Myers

How Do I Know when
a Spirit is Reaching Out to Me?

You've made the decision to adopt a spirited doll but how do you choose the right one for you? How do you know they are truly going to be happy with you?

There are a number of ways in which you will know when a spirit is reaching out to you. For some people it's very obvious. They will simply see an image of a spirited doll and immediately feel very strongly drawn towards it. People report feeling *unable to look away* or being *mesmerised* by a doll to the point that they feel they absolutely must have obtain them.

Common feelings that go along with this are:

Butterflies in the stomach.
Quickening of the heartbeat.
Tingling in your hands and toes.
An overwhelming sense of excitement.
Adrenalin rush.
Light headedness or dizziness.
Heightened emotions (it's not unusual to feel moved to tears).

For some people, however, the feeling that that a spirit is reaching out to them is more subtle. They will see an image of a spirited doll and for some time after will keep thinking about the doll or spirit. They will be going about their everyday routine when thoughts of the doll or spirit will form. It is also not uncommon to experience a physical presence in your home when a spirit is reaching for your attention. Spirits are able to come in visitation. Some believe it's to *'check out'* their prospective homes, whereas others think it's more of a plea to get your attention. People have reported seeing shadows, smelling scents, feeling watched, and have also experienced electrical interference (particularly whilst looking at the spirit dolls picture).

You may also experience more direct clues. One gentleman told us he was considering adopting a spirited doll named Arabella. In life she had loved going on cruises, loved boats and the sea. He hadn't made his mind up, and a couple of days after seeing her and reading her story, he was browsing Facebook and a photo popped up in his News Feed of a gorgeous yacht named Arabella. He said he found it odd as it is not a common name. He decided there and then that this was a sign and he adopted her.

One thing is for sure, when a spirit DOES choose you, it is inevitable. There will be no barriers, and the timing will seem perfect. The universe will ensure you both come together.

FAQs

How does a doll or object become spirited?

There are several reasons why a spirit may choose not to pass over to the other side, but to remain on our side of life. Over the years we have encountered spirits who have a personal attachment to the vessel that they are 'inhabiting' through a previous ownership (i.e. the doll or object belonged to them in life, or a child or someone they were close to). Not all spirits choose their vessel for this reason; some may have simply chosen a doll for its physical appearance. Many spirits that we have encountered have told us that the doll they have anchored to, looks very similar to how they did in life.

Spirits can also have been the subject of 'Spirit Transference' or 'Spirit Capture or Binding'. The latter is very rare and in cases where we find this we will work in partnership with various local organisations and psychic professionals to enable the spirit to freely pass over into the spirit world.

What exactly is 'attachment' or 'anchoring'?

Attachment or anchoring is when a spirit chooses to remain a part of our world, in not only a spiritual and outer body sense, but also a physical sense by attaching themselves, their energy, their thoughts, and their personalities to an object. By doing this, they anchor themselves, meaning that they have a more permanent place with us. When spirits pass over into the afterlife, it can take a long time for them to build enough energy to cross back over, which is why when loved ones die and we so desperately want a sign from them that they are okay we often don't experience anything for some time after passing.

By choosing to remain part of our world a spirit does not need to build the energy needed each time they manifest. They can feed on the energy around them (be it the energy and emotions of the living, or electrical energy, often picked up when using electromagnetic detection equipment using).

How do I know if a spirit is happy or whether they want to pass over?

You will know! If your doll comes from a reputable researcher they will have spent many weeks, months, and sometimes years studying and researching the spirit. In cases where spirits wish to pass over we assist them in order to do this. You will soon learn to pick up on the emotions and sensitivity of a spirit you welcome into your home. As you share your space and lives with them they will get to trust you, know you and respect you as you do with them. At Haunted Dolls we are always here to offer advice and support if you are concerned about your spirit adoption, whether you adopted from us or not.

Is it safe to welcome a spirit into my home if I have children or pets?

This depends entirely on the spirit. Ninety-nine per cent of spirits are very respectful of your home, and if you set ground rules, or simply communicate with them directly and let them know what's acceptable and what's not, they will abide by that. Some spirits are excellent to have around children in particular, as they can be wonderful guardians, keeping a watchful eye over those they draw close to. Some spirits, however, prefer a quieter, calmer existence than can be provided in a home with children, especially small children. We always get to know a bit about each potential adoptive family before commencing with an adoption as this is the best way to ensure adoption is successful and fulfilling for everyone. Some spirits are cheeky and playful and like to make you jump. Again, these types of spirits may not be suitable for children. When it comes to pets, animals are incredibly sensitive to the spirit world and many believe they have a sixth sense. Pets who are naturally of a nervous disposition probably will not take well to the presence of spirits; however, most animals are quite accepting and will often give you signs when your spirit is around.

Can I use my spirit doll for entertaining friends or family?

We don't recommend that spirit dolls be used as an entertainment tool, however, we do find that most spirits (once they settle in and get to know their new companions) will want to provide evidence of the paranormal and of their existence. Again this is down to the individual character of the spirit in question and when deciding whether or not to adopt we can provide answers to any questions that you have relating to an individual.

Can a spirit harm me?

The short answer here is 'No'. Part of our work involves getting to know the entity we are dealing with. Spirits cannot and do not want to harm the living; however, darker entities can create situations in which we can fall victim to bad luck and sometimes psychic attack. It's incredibly important to us to ensure that any spirit we encounter is of a 'light' nature. By this we mean they are spirits of those who were once living, had earthly bodies and can connect with us on a similar level.

It is VERY rare that we encounter dark entities. Whenever we have we have passed the responsibility over to the relevant professional bodies, either for exorcism, banishing or safe 'sealing' of an item. We never attempt to engage in communications with dark entities once their identity is established.

Tips on Communicating

1. Subtle signs.

Keep your mind, eyes and ears open for those early signs that your spirit is with you, in your home. These can vary widely from spirit to spirit but there are some usual behaviours to look out for. Electrical equipment acting strangely, i.e. TV switching channel on its own, radio coming on or going off, kettle starting to boil, lights flickering and so forth. These are all telltale signs of paranormal activity. Spirits try to reach out to us in many ways to let us know that they are there. Once you see these initial signs, it's a great time to begin helping your spirit take the next step.

2. Involve them in your life.

Okay, I don't mean take them shopping and sit them in the trolley or anything, although of course you could! No, by this I mean talk to them, tell them what are going on, how you're feeling, and any problems you're having. You will find that not only will you begin to feel closer to them by doing this, but they will also begin to warm to you, and their trust will grow. (Some spirits have been mistreated in the past, and trust may be a big issue for them. It may be that building trust is the most important thing you can do for your particular spirit.)

3. Ask for a definite sign.

If you don't ask you don't get, right? Sometimes spirits miss our cues, especially if they lived in a very different time to ours. They may see our lives as very busy and hectic and may feel their place is better in the background. Let them know you want them to share your home and want them to show themselves to you. The best time to try this for the first time is when you're alone with your doll. Dim the lights if you can, light a candle and stare into your dolls eyes. When you feel the time is right, simply ask if they are with you. Look out for those subtle signs I mentioned earlier. Does the flame of the candle flicker? Does your favourite song come on the radio? Be open to all possibilities. Not all spirits manifest into a full-bodied apparition straight away. Some don't have the energy and take time to build up to it.

4. Use gadgets.

Typical 'Ghost Hunting' gadgets can be very expensive, and in some cases you get what you pay for but in my experience I have captured some of my best EVP recordings using my old Phillips tape recorder. I now use a Phillips Digital as it's easier to upload EVPs onto the computer, but if you're not so bothered about being able to so that then tape recorders are great. It is best to leave them running as long possible and as late as you can. I find that between midnight and 3am captures the clearest EVPs from my dolls. Also, take photos! You probably do this anyway, but if you take enough photographs then sooner or later you're bound to capture something. If you have a camera that can capture thermal imaging or night vision even better! Don't forget temperature readings too. Again, these thermometers don't have to be expensive. A good digital thermometer will show you instantly if there are sudden fluctuations in the temperature of a room when you ask for a sign. If you afford one, buy an Electro Magnetic Field Reader (K2 meter). You can get these on eBay. A good combination of EVP, temperature readings, and K2 meter readings have given me the best evidence to date.

5. Be patient.

I can't emphasise enough how important it is to be patient with your spirit. Getting frustrated and creating a vortex of negative energy around your spirit will simply make them retreat. As mentioned in point two, talk to them and treat them with the respect that they deserve. Light spirits feed on positive energy. If you create a happy and harmonious environment in your home for them then they are much more likely to interact with you.

6. Keep them happy.

By this point you're probably thinking, *This seems like a lot of work!* To a degree it is. To get the most out of the relationship you will need to put in time and effort. Some spirits like to look out of a window and watch the world go by. Some like to see green space outdoors so try facing them towards the garden. Some like to be high up out of reach of animals, others like to be in the think of the action, in the lounge or kitchen for example. It may take time to establish where your spirit is happiest. Try moving them periodically; you will soon get a feel for where they want to stay.

This list is by no means exhaustive as there are many ways in which you can try to communicate with your spirit.

The Pitfalls of Being
a Paranormal Investigator

I don't think many children want to grow up to be a paranormal investigator. I don't think many children would even know what that is. So life doesn't really give us a blue print when it comes to understanding what working in this field may entail. It's not like being a doctor or teacher. There are no expectations, but also not much support.

When my hobby and obsession organically became a 'job' a few years ago, I couldn't have imagined there would be a negative side to working in the field of paranormal research. However, there are many. Of course, these pale into insignificance each time I get solid confirmation that I've contacted the 'other side', but day to day, there are stumbles and pitfalls, as with anything else.

Anyone considering taking the plunge should consider some factors carefully. Each of these factors I speak of from personal experience.

1. Ask yourself if you **TRULY** care what other people think of you.

   The subject of the afterlife, spirits, ghosts and the paranormal will always divide people. The believers will think you're wonderful, the sceptics will either think you're crazy or a fraud.

2. It's increasingly competitive.

   Like many businesses, those in the paranormal field are vulnerable. There is always someone looking to trip you up, catch you out or create a storm of negativity around your work and your claims. The difficulty, and maybe the saviour to a large extent, is that the unexplained is very subjective. I may tell you that I have had a profound experience that was very real, but for a sceptic (or a competitor) this can easily be explained away. It's this grey area that those who are threatened by you and your work will look to manipulate and use to their advantage. For this reason, if you are going to take this role seriously, you have to believe in what you're doing, and do it well. Hopefully you will reach a point where your work speaks for itself.

3. Forget working nine to five.

    You can't be a paranormal investigator nine to five. You have to allow yourself to be fully open to any and every experience around you, and be prepared to travel at short notice, or to begin recording in the middle of the night if things start to happen. When you're out on site it can get cold, boring and tiring. Of course you also get the extreme adrenalin rush that comes with paranormal experiences too, so a rollercoaster it certainly is.

4. The moral dilemma.

    Inevitably, you are likely to reach a point where you wonder if you are doing the right thing. You will have had people tell you you're dabbling in things you shouldn't, or that you should "let the dead rest", and there are only so many disapproving looks you can take, before you begin to wonder if they're right. I have often thought, maybe in doing this work, in communicating with spirits in the way that I do, I am reserving my spot in Hell. What if I shouldn't be doing this? What if God disapproves? After all, there are those who believe that all apparent paranormal experiences and communications from the afterlife are merely a trick by Satan himself, and that in 'dabbling' we are giving him access to our eternal soul. Ultimately, you need to make peace with where you sit with this.

My life, My Studies and My Beliefs

So what have I learnt over the past 16 years of investigating the paranormal? I guess two primary things:

Death is not the end of the story, only the end of the very first chapter.
There is more to life than a purely physical existence. This I know to be true. Some part of us moves onwards, or in some cases, doesn't move on at all. It remains an onlooker, overseeing those that exist in the physical sense. Some people call what remains the soul, others the spirit. I prefer to think of it as our essence. The 'thing' that remains once our bodies cease to be of use, is what makes us each unique. Exactly what happens of course is the eternal mystery and maybe part of me, in searching for answers, prefers not to delve too deeply as this will be my ultimate discovery when the time comes, and I wouldn't want to rob myself of that.

With answers come only more questions.
I entered the paranormal field so organically that it didn't even really occur to me that I had. It was like entering adulthood for me, it just kind of happened. I knew that I had a curiosity that couldn't be silenced by reading about what other people thought, and that unless I did my own exploration, I would still have questions that would remain unanswered. As time has gone on, I realize, however, that with knowledge and experience there comes a new level of curiosity. Maybe there is some natural law that prevents us being able to fully grasp what we are destined to experience in death. Maybe I simply have a questioning mind, and no amount of answers will change that.

It is important to add that in documenting my experiences in this book, I am by no means looking to convince anyone of my beliefs. I still, even now, approach each new case with a hint of scepticism. My view is that how can you effectively test any theory if you already believe it to be true? What I would ask is that you give yourself the chance to believe. The world is full of miracles, those that happen every day for all to see, and those that are only visible when you choose to look in the right places.

Testimonies

The following are actual customer testimonies from the purchasers of some of our dolls.

"It took about 2 weeks for me to really feel Elizabeth was with me. I tried her in different locations and eventually felt sure she was happy when I placed her on the windowsill in my bedroom. That night, I woke up at about 3am and I could see a figure standing by the doorway. I wasn't scared, surprisingly. I knew it was her. She smiled, then left. My home is so much more alive with her here. I have been tempted to use an Ouija board to chat to her, but have followed your advice and resisted. I know they can be dangerous. I'll keep you posted! Thanks Jayne. You're wonderful."
Jeanette Cooper, UK

"All I can say is I was a sceptic. My husband has always been a believer and got me doll for my birthday (as a half joke in a way – no offence!). Anyway, since having her here we have heard laughing, crying and sighing coming from the doll itself...seriously I'm not joking, if I listen hard I can hear it. I have also seen shadows move past me in the hallway and feel a definite presence in the house. Far from being afraid, I'm thrilled! I now know there is an afterlife, what could be better? Thanks Jayne, and thank you for being so understanding about the postage etc. I'm now looking for a second doll so let me know who is ready to be adopted!"
Julie McKeith, Glasgow, Scotland

Hi, I'd just like to say that I am so happy with Barnaby the clown doll! He is such wonderful spirit to have in my home. Well, there's nothing creepy about the guy but there is some activity as I hear footsteps – loud footsteps – coming from my bedroom where he is. I've heard it twice or more, at night or early morning. I treat him like friend and even talk to him. I think he settled well here in my home and is very peaceful here too, thanks to this awesome website! I would like to say to anyone who's thinking about buying a haunted doll from here you can't go wrong because they are REAL SPIRITS! But they must be treated with respect, thanks so much I can't wait for the next doll to come here.

Martin Rowlands, Caenarfon, North Wales

When Peter arrived I knew straight away that he was something very special, such a beautiful doll and so soft, one of those dolls that you just want to hold all of the time. But I know I had to respectfully keep my distance, after I put him on my bed (and he spread out like he owned it)…I could just feel his face…staring at me, watching me wherever I went. The doll itself hadn't moved, it was the spirit's face inside. He was moving his head and eyes to look at me and he was blinking…this took me a while to get used to as I never had it with any other spirit. Within just 3 hours of him arriving, activity started happening.

My mother kept hearing water running all over the house, she checked all of the taps but none of them were turned on, this was strange because Peter's death was actually water related. The first night that I had him I had no sleep at all. I kept hearing conversations, running water. My lips and arms kept going numb as I felt rushes of air go over me; there was also whispering. He has actually calmed down quite a lot now and kind of clung himself to me, he hugs into me whenever I hold him. These dolls are very special and very real and shouldn't really be adopted by people who are not experienced, but I'm glad I did adopt him. I love my little mischievous boy…and I hope he continues to feel as happy as

he makes me. Thank you Jayne. I wish you luck xx
Skyabell Ryde, Lincolnshire

Juliet is a very special girl; she arrived this Tuesday and already showed some activities while getting to know her. As I was talking about some bad things I've been through, she'd have this stern expression, and as I was talking to her while looking at her eye-to-eye I could've sworn her vessel was breathing. Not only that, but she also showed herself to my grandmother via dream communication. My grandmother saw Juliet smiling at her and had told me about her dream earlier. I asked her to describe the person she saw, and when I showed her Juliet she was so happy and said that the one she saw in her dreams resembles Juliet's vessel. She's started talking to Juliet too and now considers Juliet as her youngest grandchild. Thank you so much for allowing me to be the one who adopts Juliet.
Lois Francisco, Luxor, Egypt

I love my doll I recently won in a contest Jayne held, and it didn't take long for Sally to arrive for me to realize she was truly spirited. From paintings falling off the wall, dreams about her, orb photo captures, to the scent of flowers in my bedroom, she wasted no time showing me she was HERE. She is a very special doll and I continue to get activity in some form or another from her.
Brittany Benton, El Dorado, Arkansas

Wow what can I say, apart from I'm really happy that I have found Jayne's page, it's really good. Yesterday, 15/4/14, I received Amelia in the post, I'm rather impressed that it only took one day for delivery. I carefully opened Amelia and immediately I felt a warm feeling around her. We've had activity already, she seems to like my nail varnish as she had

opened my draw and removed it along with a bottle of perfume, bless her. I love her to bits, and I feel a strong bond already... She will be very happy with us here as I will treasure her.
Sharon Brown, UK

As a retired detective after many years, I'm quite sceptical when it comes to non-existing evidence to what can be discerned as a natural phenomenon, yet, how can I explain what I am about to share:

I was interested in purchasing an alleged "haunted doll" just to see what would happen, after filling out an "adoption form" and giving Jayne additional information about us. I received an email one Friday morning that she has a doll for sale that she believed would be a good fit for us. Apparently the doll "reached out" to Jayne when she was sleeping and she "dreamed" about her being meant for us. In Jayne's email she told me the history of the spirit whose name is "Arabella". "What a strange name," I wrote back. "I've never heard of that name before!" Jayne's answer was that it was more common back in the 19th century when this spirit lived. A couple minutes after I received her email, I started to roam on FB and visited my friend's page. Still in the police, he posted a short clip of himself on the job. I then decided to check the people who "liked" the clip and randomly hit on one and what came up caused me to gasp: This person, who I do not know and randomly just opened his Facebook page, had a picture of a yacht as his background photo. Guess what the name of the yacht is: Arabella! What are the coincidence of something like that happening? As Jayne wrote back, Arabella apparently was reaching out to me! Needless to say, she was purchased, we have experienced minor noise in the room when no one is around and some shadows out of the corner of our eyes, waiting for more!

Thank you Jayne for being authentic!
Elie Fagan, Maryland, USA

"I haven't even received my doll yet but already I have seen the spirits shadow at the foot of my bed. My friend saw it also. I guess she is here already!"
Kristabelle Dione, USA

"Tina has settled in nicely, we have been tracking her movements around the house with an EMF visual meter. Then last night we set up a candle, her geode's beside her and she answered 4 or 5 questions moving the pendulum, and the ghost meter beeped rapidly and was going off big time. Tina is real and is here, I'm very impressed with your studies and the confirmation of what a pleasure she is to have here. Nothing creepy, scary or annoying at all.

I was so impressed as soon as I opened the box to release her I gave her presents. We treat her like our daughter, and she is real without a doubt. The feeling of positive energy in this house is amazing ever since she arrived. The communication last night was just so moving, her middle name is Marie and we're going to try to get her last name next time she talks to us. Amazing, it's beyond my expectations really. You're a pro, she is the perfect fit for us but you knew it all along, very impressive you are, my dear!"
John Foster, Canada

"My Tammy Lynne never ceases to amaze me! I have seen her several times walking around our house after I told her to never be afraid to be herself and to feel free to check out her new home.

She pops into my mind to tell me things (which is something I've never experienced before with any of my other spirit family). Her doll's face and expression changes, she puts out a feeling of extreme love and calm, has bonded with my cat, and when I pick her up her energy sends tingles up my hands and arms. (A friend of mine has also experienced this to the point of goose bumps on her skin.)

My Tammy Lynne is truly amazing and we are so grateful for being brought together.

Much love. Tam and Tammy Lynne (Lynette)."

Tamara Barron, Australia

Bobby has recently arrived with his new owner who is a medium and palm reader based in the US. She claims that he is her most active spirit doll.

"Let me say, that I have never experienced the communication from a spirit that has been outside of my family, the way I have with Bobby. Before he even was shipped, and during his trip here, I had activity nightly in my bedroom and I knew it was him because the other spirits sharing my home know the rules. But last night I had an interesting dream in which I believe my deceased father took me to meet Bobby. As I am typing out the vivid details of the dream I hear the postman and stop, and who should be at my door? BOBBY! Also amazingly, I felt his energy through the box, and upon opening the box, the energy shifted in the room and when I touched him, I became dizzy, light headed and again needed to quickly ground! This is THE strongest physical sensations I have ever felt from a spirit outside of my family! I LOVE HIM! And thank you so much again Jayne! I will continue to update, but now I must take some time with him and give him a proper welcoming!"

Rahjeena Drabarni, California, USA

References

This book could not have been completed without the help and information provided by the sources below. Both of the authors wish to extend their thanks to the authors and originators of the following resources:

True hauntings by Peter Haining Robinson,2008

Oddee.com.
http://www.oddee.com/item_98684.aspx
Mysterious Universe.
http://mysteriousuniverse.org/2013/07/true-tales-of-haunted-dolls/
Ehow.com.
http://www.ehow.com/how-does_5535309_meter-work.html - k2
Westnorfolkparanormal.com.
http://www.westnorfolkparanormal.com/emf.php
Examiner.com.
http://www.examiner.com/article/ghost-hunting-101-what-is-a-k-ii-meter-and-how-do-i-use-it
Malkuthsghost.com.
http://www.malkuthsghost.com/2009/08/how-to-use-pendulum.html
Ghost101.com.
http://ghosts101.com/pendulums-how-they-work-and-how-to-use-them
The Worry Depository.
http://www.tc.umn.edu/~mcdo0151/legend.html
Aboutentertainment.com.
http://paranormal.about.com/od/ghostaudiovideo/a/All-About-EVP.htm

Magic, Spells and Potions.
  http://magic-spells-and-potions.com/magical_properties_of_
  salt_protection_purification_healing.htm
Amanda Linette Meder.
  http://amandalinettemeder.com/blog/2013/9/26/benefits-and-
  uses-of-white-sage#.VAdhQmOx3w0=
Delaware Paranormal.
  http://delawareparanormal.blogspot.co.uk/2012/10/haunted-
  objects.html
Surlalune Fairytales.com.
  http://www.surlalunefairytales.com
Studies in vodoun.
  http://thelifeandtimesofanecclecticfreak.blogspot.co.uk/
  2007/03/how-voodoo-works-by-tracy-v.html
Tsukumogami.
  http://en.wikipedia.org/wiki/Tsukumogami

About the Authors

Jayne has had a fascination with all things paranormal for as long as she can remember. She began studying the paranormal as a hobby in 2001. With qualifications in criminology, psychology and counselling, Jayne loves continuously learning and gaining knowledge, and is currently studying demonology alongside working towards a recognised qualification in paranormal investigation.

Her favourite haunted location is Greyfriars Kirkyard in Edinburgh.

Award winning author Dan Weatherer (also known as Father Darkness) was first discovered and published by *Haunted Magazine* in spring, 2013. His first tale 'The Legend of the Chained Oak' was an immediate success and was made into a short film which won the award for **'Best Horror'** at the **Portobello Film Festival** and also the **'Best UK Short Film'** award at the **Bram Stoker International Film Festival** and the **Stoke Your Fires Film Festival** 2014.

Aside from the publication of numerous short stories with a multitude of presses, his next major project was a solo collection of short stories titled *The Soul That Screamed* (Winner of the Preditors & Editors™ Readers' Poll 'Best Anthology 2013'.)

He also occasionally writes short stories for children. 'Gilbert's Well' and 'A Quest for Noah' have both appeared in charity anthologies.

His second collection *Only The Good Burn Bright* is complete and will be available soon.

Dan is also an official member of the **Horror Writers Association.**

BOOKS

6th Books investigates the paranormal, supernatural, explainable or unexplainable. Titles cover everything included within parapsychology: how to, lifestyles, beliefs, myths, theories and memoir.